People of Plenty

People of Plenty

*Economic Abundance
and the American Character*

By DAVID M. POTTER

 THE UNIVERSITY OF CHICAGO PRESS

CHARLES R. WALGREEN FOUNDATION LECTURES

THE UNIVERSITY OF CHICAGO PRESS, CHICAGO & LONDON
The University of Toronto Press, Toronto 5, Canada

Published 1954. Third Impression 1962. Composed and printed by
THE UNIVERSITY OF CHICAGO PRESS, *Chicago, Illinois, U.S.A.*

TO DILYS

Foreword

This volume is based upon lectures given at the University of Chicago in the autumn of 1950 under the auspices of the Charles R. Walgreen Foundation for the Study of American Institutions. In it Professor Potter singles out from among the many concepts and situations that in one manner or another affect our ways of thinking and living the importance of the fundamental American belief in this country as a land of plenty and of golden opportunity. In lively fashion he shows the influence of this hopeful creed on our politics; on our attitude toward democracy, economic problems, and business; and on our newly espoused world outlook. This is a basic study of American society, and it should contribute to a better understanding of Americans by Americans and of Americans by people in other lands.

JEROME G. KERWIN

Chairman, Charles R. Walgreen Foundation
for the Study of American Institutions

Acknowledgments

Like most writers, I would be very much at a loss if I were under compulsion to weigh exactly what other writers, living and dead, have contributed to my efforts. In common with academic authors in general, I am able to go only a few steps beyond the point to which others have brought me. My footnotes indicate many of the writers whose work I have relied upon and whose ideas have helped me. Yet the nature of this kind of obligation is complex, and everyone who has engaged in activity of this kind will understand that sometimes the authors whom I cite conspicuously are essentially witnesses whom I looked up to support ideas which had already come to me by some other channel, while others whom I do not name and of whom perhaps I am scarcely conscious may have indirectly provided the catalysts of my thought.

Compared with the indirect and complex problem of the derivation of ideas in the cosmic sense, the question of personal obligation in these matters is relatively direct and simple, for the writer, if he is lucky, can always count the names of certain friends and men of good will who have aided him in such direct, palpable, generous, and unselfish fashion that he knows without question that they helped him to write his book. There were a number who so helped me, and I am happy to thank William O. Aydelotte and Ralph E. Turner for helpful comment on the first two chapters; Frank M. Johnson for suggestions which prompted me to develop certain points in chapter iii; John Sirjamaki for valuable criticisms on chapter iv; Arthur Schlesinger, Jr., for ideas relating to chapter v and the final chapter; Robert H. L. Wheeler for very helpful points on chapters vi and viii; George W. Pierson for expert and valuable suggestions on chapter vii; and Eugene Davidson, Norman Donaldson, Norman Holmes Pearson, and Cushing Strout for helping me in various ways with my treatment of advertising.

For general comment on the manuscript as a whole, I have had the advantage of suggestions by Richard S. and Katherine S. W. Barnes. William H. Jordy read the entire manuscript, giving me both encouragement and specific suggestions which helped substantially. David Riesman wrote an over-all criticism which was generous and at the same time searching, and from which I benefited a great deal. Finally, Paul Pickrel has, at one time or another, been over most of the manuscript twice. He edited two of the chapters which were published in the *Yale Review* (chap. viii almost as it stands and chap. v very much altered), but his criticisms on the other parts were almost as thorough as on these two. His incisive criticisms in detail and his wise general suggestions have been immensely valuable to me.

I am grateful to the Walgreen Foundation for an invitation to lecture, which prompted me to undertake this study in the first place, and to Jerome G. Kerwin and the editors of the University of Chicago Press for the patience, kindness, and skill with which they have helped me to bring the material at last to the point of publication.

Table of Contents

Introduction: History, the Behaviorial Studies, and the Science of Man

In the summer of 1950, under the stimulus of an invitation from the Walgreen Foundation, I embarked upon the seemingly innocent task of writing six lectures on the American character, and especially on the influence of American economic abundance upon this character. The theme itself was certainly a wide-open one, and nobody capable of arranging words on paper has ever been required to show any further credentials before offering vast generalizations on the American, this "new man," as Crèvecœur called him. My original purpose, therefore, was only to join the mixed lot of scholars, maiden ladies, itinerant lecturers, professional pundits, and overnight experts whose writings have adorned this subject. As I moved into the inquiry, however, I was assailed by misgivings as to the validity of the whole concept of "national character," and, as I burrowed into the literature relating to it, I was embarrassed, as a historian, to discover that the most telling contributions, in my opinion, came from cultural anthropologists and social psychologists rather than from my fellow-historians.

After a while, the problems of establishing a valid concept of national character and of seeking some possible links between the work done by historians and by behavioral scientists in this field began to seem more important than the specific problem of the influence of economic abundance upon the American character. Yet, at the same time, it remained true that my primary purpose was to examine the operation of this economic factor in the development of American life. First one aspect has seemed to predominate and then the other, and I am at last left in uncertainty as to which side is heads and which side tails on my own coin. One can read this volume as a theoretical study of the conceptual problem of national character and of the relationships between history and the behavioral sciences, regarding the chapters on abundance and its influence in America as merely illustrative; or one can read it as the concrete study of the impact of one tangible factor upon the character of the American people, regarding the opening sections on historical and behavioral approaches to national character simply as a framework necessary for fixing the material on America in its proper logical place in the literature of the subject. I am keenly aware that by thus writing a book of a dualistic nature I expose myself to the inevitable gambit of the reviewer: that the portion on which he is expert really will not do at all but that the other part appears rather interesting. Perhaps I will be fortunate if each part is not compared unfavorably with the other.

In any event, it seems valid to begin by recognizing that generalization about national character is only a special case of the larger practice of generalization about human groups of any kind. There are just a few branches of learning which attempt this kind of generalization, and history was, for many centuries, the only one. But today there are several, and it may be well to start with a consideration of the way in which these various disciplines have approached this part of their responsibility in the study of man.

Of all the branches of learning cultivated by man, there is probably none which deals with a greater body of data than does history. The task of history, to record all that is significant in human experience, for many centuries and many lands, has implied such an immense responsibility, and one of such immediacy, that it has engendered in historians an almost obsessive drive to get on with the job, to start marshaling the data, to begin straightening out the detailed and complex factual questions with which the record abounds. Consequently, history has become preeminently a concrete and "practical" subject, with but little attention to philosophical or theoretical aspects. Occasionally, some aberrant historian has paused to consider the philosophy of history, the problem of historical causation, the existence of laws of history, or the like, but the rank and file of historians have never paid very patient attention to these speculations. With mutterings about "work to do," they have quickly turned back to their busyness with deeds and events. As for historical interpretation, they have often disclaimed any such function, insisting that the facts alone would answer the historian's questions and never recognizing that these questions themselves, like fishers' nets, might profoundly influence the character of the facts which would be caught in the haul.

This preoccupation with fact, coupled as it was with a rough-and-ready willingness to tackle the most profound problems of society, has been the principal glory and, at the same time, the major weakness of history as a branch of learning. The glory, because history has dared to seek the answers to questions which other disciplines would have declined for the lack of an adequate method. History has never held itself aloof from life or guarded its own purity by confining itself to topics for which it possessed a fully tested methodological and conceptual apparatus of attack. It has never permitted the tyranny of method to dictate the subjects which it would investigate and has never shifted its attention from men to mice because of the seductive fact that mice lend themselves to precise investigation more readily than do men. It has also been the glory of history that its professional devotees have never entirely lost communication with the intelligent layman, as the practitioners of the social sciences have almost universally done. The language of history has never become divorced from the common speech, and the historian has scarcely been touched by the baneful belief that it would lower his professional standards to write in plain terms which any man might understand. In a democracy which depends upon men of learning to provide the ordinary man with sound information for dealing with public affairs, the historian is almost the only kind of scholar who has fulfilled the responsibility of speaking directly to the people.

But if history may claim these glories, it must also admit the serious defects implicit in its merits. In its headlong, *ad hoc* assault upon the record of human experience, history has built its narrative upon an extraordinary mélange of unstated premises, random assumptions, untested hypotheses, and miscellaneous notions about the nature of man, the workings of society, and the causation of historical change. The anomalous nature of this conceptual foundation has scarcely been recognized by historians, much less confronted by them, and thus they have written with assurance about the distinctive character of individual persons or groups of men, without having reached any agreement as to the nature of man in general; they have traced the course of history as a fight for human freedom, although no one has ever proved that humanity really prefers freedom to security; they have enumerated the "causes" of countless wars, without ever coming to an understanding about the causation of war in general; and they have described the process by which nationalism reshaped the modern world, without being sure what they mean by "nationalism."[1]

Unfortunately, this lack of precision in evaluating or defining the basic elements betrayed itself most glaringly in connection with the one factor which remains central throughout all history —namely, the human factor. The very term "history" means, in fact, human history, and the whole record of history is, in a sense, an account of dynamic external forces operating upon men and of the reactions and responses of men to these forces. For such an account, therefore, it would seem obviously necessary to take an analytical view both of the dynamic factors which have operated and of the human receptors—either individual men

1. Karl W. Deutsch, *Nationalism and Social Communication* (Boston: Technology Press of the Massachusetts Institute of Technology; New York: John Wiley & Sons, Inc., 1953), pp. 3–14.

or individual societies—upon which these factors have had their impact. Yet it is a curious fact that the same analytical standards were not applied on both sides of the equation, and scholars who would never have dreamed of discussing the influence of geography upon man without taking a scientific approach to geography apparently felt no obligation to take a scientific approach to man. This has been conspicuously true, for instance, in the literature dealing with the American frontier, where fairly refined study has been given to the precise nature of the different attractions which drew men to the frontier at various stages, but little attention has been accorded to the differential character of diverse human groups—the French as contrasted with the Anglo-Americans, or twentieth-century Americans as contrasted with nineteenth-century Americans—which made some groups highly responsive and some relatively unresponsive to frontier attractions.

At times it has even appeared that historians could not arrive at a settled conception as to the nature of man, for at various times they have harbored a wide range of unstated and unconsidered assumptions about the human creature. Orthodox historians regarded him as a being made in the image of God and endowed with an immortal soul; materialistic ones regarded him as a mammal tortured by the attempt to transcend his own animal nature. Democrats postulated his capacity to think for himself and his equality with other men. Economists accepted as an axiom the belief that he would always be guided by enlightened self-interest. Liberals pictured the yearning for freedom as one of his basic drives. Calvinists believed him to be born sinful but liable to regeneration through God's grace, while romantics believed him to be born virtuous but liable to corruption through the evils of society. The mid-nineteenth century, as Ralph H. Gabriel has remarked, confidently explained him in terms of a double triad: "He was body, mind, and soul, and his mind consisted of emotions, intellect, and will." When historians wrote about the history of man, they seldom paused to specify whether the protagonist of their tale was one of the types named above or was some other fellow altogether.[2]

If history failed to grapple effectively with the problem of man and his nature, this was very largely because the study of man requires the derivation of general or abstract conclusions from a mass of concrete human data, and history for nearly twenty-five centuries after the time of Herodotus simply did not deal in generalization. It dealt with unique events, such as the conduct of a particular battle or the negotiation of a particular treaty, and all of the much-vaunted "historical method" was a method for determining specific events by means of rigorous textual criticism and severe rules for the evaluation of evidence. The arts or techniques of broad interpretation or of generalization from a mass of specific data were not part of the "historical method," even though historians might engage freely in interpretations and generalizations based on their personal judgment as individuals. In recent decades, as history has turned increasingly to the treatment of social and economic themes, such as changes in ideas or morals, the relations between diverse social classes, or the operation of economic forces upon society, the historian's lack of systematic procedure in the practice of generalization has become a serious liability. But the force of tradition is so

2. "The study of history and politics is primarily the study of men, and . . . all political theory and political science must begin with a clear view of the psychology of man, at least in certain aspects of his behaviour. All the great and effective political theorists have recognised this. Hobbes began his political theory with a psychological theory—his mechanical, despotic state was devised for a mechanical, fear-driven humanity. John Locke and his eighteenth-century followers advocated political freedom—*i.e.* non-intervention by government—on the assumption that man was naturally good and self-improving and that his economic activities were naturally helpful to society; while the seventeenth-century philosophers whom he challenged had proceeded from an opposite assumption. The same point can be made indefinitely. Political theory which does not start from a theory of man is in my view quite worthless" (Hugh Trevor-Roper, "Human Nature in Politics," *The Listener,* December 10, 1953), pp. 993–94.

strong that this deficiency has scarcely even been recognized by writers on historical method, and certainly no serious steps have been taken to correct it. This observation, however, is somewhat aside from the point, and all that needs to be said for purposes of this discussion is that although history has constantly made all sorts of assumptions about the nature of man, it has never possessed any systematic method for checking these assumptions. In a sense, this is equivalent to saying that historical method has not included any means for analysis of the chief factor with which history deals.

In making these observations upon the increasingly conspicuous deficiencies of historical scholarship, I do not by any means intend to suggest that historians have failed in their task as recorders of human experience. On the contrary, historical analysis and historical writing have improved immeasurably over the last two centuries and also over the last two decades. But I do mean to suggest that the achievements of historians have been made largely through the exercise of common sense and individual sagacity, in spite of the defective methodological and conceptual foundation upon which their work has been erected. And I mean especially to argue that this deficiency has shown itself most acutely in the historian's failure to take an analytical view of the one factor which is present in all history—namely, the human factor, both in its singular manifestation, where it involves the individual man, or in its group manifestation, where it involves society.

For many centuries historians held almost exclusive jurisdiction over the applied study of man. It is not without significance that in ancient times, when the nine Muses presided over the arts and sciences, Clio, and Clio alone, held sway in the area where the social sciences now flourish. This remained true until very recent times, and even when economics and political science developed, they did not scrutinize human behavior but instead assumed the existence of an "economic man" or a "political animal" or an individual in a state of "nature" (the state of nature most favored by economists was a desert island occupied by economic men in a number not greater than could be counted on the fingers of one hand). These creatures, it was supposed, would act automatically in accordance with the laws of economic or political reason rather than in accordance with the uncharted workings of human psychology. Therefore, the actual conduct of the human creature was left almost entirely to be recorded by history, and one might say that history retained this monopoly for two and a half millenniums—from Herodotus to Sigmund Freud.

So long as history retained sole custody of the study of human conduct, the extent of its omissions was the measure of what remained neglected. But the past few decades have witnessed the rapid growth of a group of behavioral sciences which have moved in to fill the vacuum, and these new sciences have developed so rapidly that the late Ralph Linton felt justified in declaring in 1943 that "it seems safe to say that the next few years will witness the emergence of a science of human behavior."[3]

The branches of learning which Linton visualized as converging to produce a science of human behavior and which are now customarily designated as the "behavioral sciences" are three in number. First, psychology, with a focus primarily upon the individual, concerns itself with human drives, motivation, and conditioning and contributes insight into the way in which "the deeper levels of personality are conditioned by environmental factors." Second, sociology, with a focus primarily upon the group, concerns itself with the complex structure of society and provides a basis for the understanding of interpersonal relations, which are vital in the formation of personality and which cannot be understood "except with reference to the positions which

3. *The Cultural Background of Personality* (New York: D. Appleton-Century Co., 1945), p. 5. The quoted passages in the paragraph that follows are from this volume (pp. xvi, xvii, 5, 19).

the individuals involved occupy in the structural system of their society." Third, anthropology, through its scrutiny of diverse societies, gives a certain perspective to the study of human behavior, and, through its concept of culture—"the way of life of any society," the pattern of "organized repetitive responses of a society's members"—it provides a key to the continuity of society, to the socializing of the individual, and to the differentiation of personality patterns and group behavior in diverse societies.

The development of the behavioral sciences and their convergence in a science of human behavior hold great potential importance for history. These new studies displace history as the primary study of man. They are moving, perhaps imperfectly, but certainly purposefully, to resolve those basic questions about the nature of man and his society which history has not only failed to answer but has often failed even to recognize or to define. They are formulating concepts, such as that of "culture," which the historian may on occasion use with great advantage. Of these facts we may be sure.

But as to the broader relationship between history and the behavioral sciences, there is no such assurance. Certainly history has not been, and cannot and should not be, regarded as one of the cluster which make up the behavioral group. Probably it cannot even operate in close relationship with them. But the contiguity of the two in dealing, perhaps at different levels, with aspects of human experience, must hold important implications for each which have not been explored on either side. Linton offered a clue to the meaning of history for the study of culture when he declared that "culture is the precipitate of history"; but, on the whole, he left this suggestion undeveloped. Caroline Ware has broken ground for a consideration of the meaning of the culture concept to the study of history in her symposium on *The Cultural Approach to History* (1949), which grew out of a session at the meeting of the American Historical Association in 1948. But historians, generally, failed to take their cues from her study.

Even in advance of specific efforts to bring history and the behavioral sciences into conjunction, however, one can anticipate certain valuable results. History can learn much about the nature of man and society from the behavioral sciences; the behavioral sciences can learn much about what may be called the "external forces impinging upon man," and about the nature of social change, from history. The value to history of a more precise understanding of the nature of man is too obvious to require elaboration, but it may be noted that historians at present attempt to treat the history of particular ideas, without any adequate recognition of the individual personalities and the cultural contexts within which these ideas are rooted; they constantly attempt to assess the motivation of men in such specific acts as going to war or initiating economic aggression, without possessing adequate knowledge of the general principles and complexities of human motivation; and they attempt to account for the rise and fall of civilizations without any systematic inquiry into what conditions are requisite for the effective operation of society and what ones are detrimental. The potential value to the behavioral sciences, on the other hand, of a more active awareness of historical forces, is suggested by the fact that the behavioral sciences, and especially cultural anthropology, have scored their greatest successes in dealing with so-called "primitive" societies and have encountered storms of controversy when they turned their focus upon Western man, in America or elsewhere. There are, no doubt, several reasons for this, including our own reluctance to be clinically dissected by the cultural anthropologist; but certainly one of the foremost reasons is that primitive societies present relatively static cultures, and the existence of these cultures in a state of equilibrium makes it possible to explain the society in terms of the culture, without reference to historic forces. Modern Western society, however, presents a culture or cultures in a state of fairly rapid change; therefore, society cannot be explained except in terms of the process of change, and the concept of culture provides no means for such an explanation, without the aid of history. It is not the "simplicity," as one might loosely suppose, of primitive societies which has made them easier for the anthropologist to explain, for they are, in fact, not simple, as he will be the first to agree. It is the absence of rapid or significant change, and the consequent opportunity to work without using the one study that deals with social change, which is history. Indeed, if there is any one subject with which history is concerned, that subject is change—how things ceased to be as they had been before, how they became what they had not been.

But though one might hope to obtain fairly ready agreement to these observations, it still remains for scholars from both sides to explore this highly important and seldom-crossed frontier between history and the behavioral sciences.

Although I had no original inclination to explore along this frontier and have no special qualifications to do so, my attempt to come to grips with the problem of national character brought me inadvertently into this zone where history and the behavioral sciences meet. For history has much to say about the differentiation of the traits of a single large group of people from the traits of people in other groups, and the behavioral sciences have also. When the historian observes this differentiation, he is prone to speak, perhaps very imprecisely, of "national character." When the behavioral scientist observes it, he talks of "culture patterns" and "personality norms." But in many cases they are speaking of the same thing. Therefore, it seemed impossible to go ahead with my inquiry without examining at least one segment of this frontier and observing the interplay between history and the behavioral sciences as they operated within this segment. This, of course, led to a question what possible significance history and these new sciences might hold for one another or at least how they might reinforce one another in dealing with the subject at hand.

Although only the first two chapters of this book were written for the express purpose of considering the relationship between history and the behavioral sciences, the reader will find, I hope, that the workings of this relationship are in evidence throughout the volume, and it may be worth while at this point to foreshadow the sequence in which the subject will be developed. I propose to show in my first chapter how the concept of national character has been employed in the writing of history, how important a place it has had in historical thought, and how historians have used and abused the concept. I will also attempt to indicate what part it had in the shaping of historical thought and how it has fallen into a certain measure of disrepute among historians, mostly because of the abuses to which it was put and the carelessness with which it was handled. In my second chapter I propose to show how the behavioral scientists are handling the same concept today: how they have refined it by a systematic consideration of what constitutes a group in the large sense (whether designated as a "culture," or as a "nation"); how their concept of culture provided a tenable explanation for the existence of national character after the traditional explanation in racist terms had become untenable; and how the behavioral scientists' concept of the secondary environment has given a new orientation to the study of environmental factors. Instead of dealing with this abstractly, I shall discuss at some length the way in which certain outstanding behavioral scientists have treated the American character, what they conceive this character to be, and how they account for it.

Thus far, my discussion will have dealt primarily with what the behavioral sciences can contribute to history. But in the ensuing chapters, I shall turn to the question of what history can contribute in the treatment of subjects with which the behavioral sciences are concerned. As I shall show, those behavioral scientists who have written on the American character have attempted to account for their cultural findings by means of explanations which are essentially historical, and, as I shall argue, these historical explanations are not entirely satisfactory. This circumstance would in itself argue a larger function for history. But instead of offering mere negative criticism, I shall also attempt, over several chapters, a fairly extended analysis of the influence of a single factor which is certainly historical in its character but which, I hope to demonstrate, has had important effects as a "precipitant" (to use Linton's term) of the culture. This factor is the unusual plenty of available goods or other usable wealth which has prevailed in America—what I shall call "economic abundance." In a general way, this factor has long been recognized as exercising an important influence upon the life and attitudes of the American people, but it has never received systematic consideration, not even in such limited form as I shall apply. It is certainly a factor which falls within the province of the historian. No one but an economist would contest for it, and certainly a behavioral scientist would not. Yet this historical factor has impinged upon the culture in innumerable ways, a few of which I shall attempt to show. After the nature of abundance as a factor has been discussed in chapter iii, chapter iv, in dealing with abundance, mobility, and status, will consider the manner in which abundance has remade the social structure within which the "status roles" and "interpersonal relations," so important to the behavioral scientist, are formed. Chapter v will consider American political behavior and political values as they have been influenced by abundance and will seek to show how abundance has given to the concept of "democracy" a distinctive meaning in America which sets it apart from democracy in other parts of the world. The sixth chapter relates to the behavior of the American people in matters of foreign policy, and it suggests that their failure to recognize the role of abundance as a contributory factor to the American way of life (or "precipitant of the American culture," as a behavioral scientist might say) has led to certain miscalculations in their effort to transmit this way of life to other peoples. Chapter vii examines what has been the historian's classic explanation of distinctiveness in the American character, namely, the influence of the frontier, and it suggests that the frontier was perhaps only one phase or one manifestation of the factor of abundance. Many of the traits which were attributed to the frontier influence, it is argued, could equally well be accounted for by the impact of abundance, and thus abundance, rather than the frontier, is proposed as the historical precipitant which produces what have been regarded as frontier aspects of American culture. Chapter viii deals with the impact of abundance in shaping one of the major institutions which guide the individual in the orientation of his values and thus ultimately play a basic part in the formation of the personality: this is national advertising, with all that its existence implies concerning the transition from a society oriented to production to one oriented to consumption. Finally, chapter ix will return to the problem of character formation as the behavioral scientist sees it and will attempt to show the effect of this historical factor upon conditions basic to the rearing of the American child.

If these analyses can stand up under criticism, it is my hope that they may help to foster a greater readiness on the part of both the historian and the behavioral scientist to make use of each other's findings. The possibility that these two could be of appreciable help to one another has not received much attention, despite the present academic zeal for interdisciplinary study and co-operative effort across departmental lines. Yet it is evident that history ought to observe very closely the progress of any science which can help to explain the nature of the actors in the historical drama. It is also evident that, though behavioral scientists may use the culture to explain human behavior, they must rely upon history to explain the culture. Although the practitioners of this oldest and these newest of disciplines may not be very congenial academic teammates, the fact remains that, if they are ever to scale the heights on which they hope to find a science of man, they must go roped together like other mountaineers.

PART I

The Study of National Character

I. The Historians and National Character

After remaining for ages almost entirely in the hands of historians, the study of national character has recently undergone a transformation which illustrates the strangeness of the tricks that time can play: it has passed very largely into the hands of medical men. Of this extraordinary development I shall have more to say later, but at the very outset it seems appropriate to note that this subject which has so recently been returned to the care of the physicians began with a physician in the first place. The earliest recorded disquisition on national character was put in writing in the fifth century before Christ by that distinguished medical practitioner, Hippocrates. In part he said: "The chief reason why Asiatics are less warlike and more gentle in character than Europeans is the uniformity of the seasons, which show no violent changes. . . . For there occur no mental shocks [to the people] . . . which are more likely to steel the temper and impart to it a fierce passion than is monotonous sameness. For it is changes of all things that rouse the temper of man and prevent its stagnation. For these reasons, I think, Asiatics are feeble. Their institutions are a contributory cause, the greater part of Asia being governed by kings. Now where men are not their own masters and independent, . . . they are not keen on military efficiency. . . . All their worthy, brave deeds merely serve to aggrandize . . . their lords while the harvest they themselves reap is danger and death. . . . [But] all the inhabitants of Asia, whether Greek or non-Greek, who are not ruled by despots, but are independent, toiling for their own advantage, are the most warlike of all men. For it is for their own sakes that they run their risks, and in their own persons do they receive the prizes of their valour as likewise the penalty of their cowardice."[1]

It seems valid to regard Hippocrates as the first writer on the subject of national character, because he approached it consciously as a problem of generalization about groups of people, while other writers did not do this. But even a few years earlier than Hippocrates, Herodotus had offered some comments in very much the same vein on the character of the Athenians. Their history, he suggested, was proof "that equality is a good thing," for "while they were under despotic rulers the Athenians were no better in war than any of their neighbours, yet once they got quit of despots they were far and away the first of all. This, then, shows that while they were oppressed they willed to be cravens, as men working for a master, but when they were freed, each one was zealous to achieve for himself."[2]

With that extraordinarily modern outlook so often evident in the Greeks, Hippocrates and Herodotus had, for a moment, anticipated the concepts of behavioral scientists twenty-five centuries later. These scientists were to make close analysis of the effects of oppression, caste, and authoritarian control upon personality and were to emerge with findings not unlike those of the Greek physician and the Greek historian.

Although these are apparently the earliest statements about national character that have survived from ancient times, it would be a mistake to exaggerate either the priority of these writers in originating the concept or their influence in the later development of the idea. For the practice of attributing group characteristics to bodies of people is apparently as old as the sense of group identity itself—that is, it is an aspect of ethnocentrism—and the countless subsequent expressions of such generalization have been

1. Hippocrates *Airs, Waters, Places*, trans. W. H. S. Jones (Loeb Classical Library, 1923), 16.

2. Herodotus *History*, trans. A. D. Godley (Loeb Classical Library, 1922–31), v. 78.

voiced as freely by the ignorant as by the readers of Greek literature.

Within the sequence of literature itself the influence of these writers was very largely neutralized, if not completely dissipated, by the writings, during the following century, of Aristotle, on the same subject. Whereas Hippocrates and Herodotus had recognized that character would change with changing conditions, such as varying degrees of authoritarianism, Aristotle presented it as fixed and unchanging. It must be said to his credit that he did not make the error of supposing that character remains constant because it is inherited in the genes—he was not a racist—but he did stress the impact of permanent conditions of climate which would cause permanent traits of character. Moreover, he extended the concept of character differences to involve not only the idea of dissimilarities but also that of inequalities, for he conceived of the Hellenic people as having the capacity of ruling the world if they could be united into one state.[3] These ideas

3. Aristotle *Politics*, trans. Benjamin Jowett (1885): "Those who live in a cold climate and in [northern] Europe are full of spirit, but wanting in intelligence and skill; and therefore they keep their freedom, but have no political organization, and are incapable of ruling over others. Whereas the natives of Asia are intelligent and inventive, but they are wanting in spirit, and therefore they are always in a state of subjection and slavery. But the Hellenic race, which is situated between them, is likewise intermediate in character, being high-spirited and also intelligent. Hence it continues free, and is the best-governed of any nation, and, if it could be formed into one state, would be able to rule the world. There are also similar differences in the different tribes of Hellas; for some of them are of a one-sided nature, and are intelligent or courageous only, while in others there is a happy combination of both qualities" (vii. 7).

Jowett calls attention in his notes to a comparable passage in Plato *Republic*, trans. Jowett, speaking of "the principles and habits which there are in the State.... Take the quality of passion or spirit;—it would be ridiculous to imagine that this quality, which is characteristic of the Thracians, Scythians, and in general of the northern nations, when found in States, does not originate in the individuals who compose them; and the same may be said of the love of knowledge, which is the special characteristic of our part of the world, or the love of money, which may, with equal truth, be attributed to the Phoenicians and Egyptians" (iv. 435–36).

of the immutability of national character and of the superiority of the peoples of a given character group have, unfortunately, shown as much vigor as did the idea that distinctive character may evolve where distinctive conditions are at work.

These theories of the distinctiveness of the character of various peoples have gained singularly ready and widespread acceptance at the hands of writers in every country and in every age. The ease with which such beliefs have won adoption requires some explanation, and I shall return to this problem a little later. Meanwhile, it may be said that probably no other class of writers has trafficked in this concept of national character so heavily as have historians. The theme of the historian almost invariably has been the story of a specific people or a specific country, and historians have found in the theory of national character a basic device for differentiating their particular subjects and, very often, for attributing special virtues to the people of whom they write. If this was true before the advent of modern nationalism, it has been vastly more so since then, when, in the case of writers like Treitschke in Germany, Lamartine in France, or Bancroft in the United States, national glorification has been the essential function of history, and the recognition of national traits has been the means for demonstrating national superiority. Among the nationalist historians, including many who avoided the extremes of chauvinism, the concept of national character became, therefore, the one dominant historical assumption which pervaded the treatment of all their material.

The extent to which historians have relied upon this assumption could probably be illustrated from the historical literature of any country, but, since I am personally most familiar with the American branch of the literature and since other parts of this book deal with the question of American national character, it may be well to draw upon American history for an illustration and to recognize how widely the concept of a distinctive American character has been adopted by American historians.

Among the more prominent American historical writers, there is hardly one who does not, either occasionally or constantly, explicitly or implicitly, invoke the idea of an American national character. Without attempting to be thorough, one may easily note a few examples. Henry Steele Commager tells us that it cannot be doubted that "by some alchemy, out of the blending of inheritance, environment, and experience, there came a distinctive American character." Allan Nevins, in his *Ordeal of the Union*, begins by delineating "the virtues and vices of the national character," as it manifested itself at the middle of the nineteenth century. Arthur M. Schlesinger has devoted one of his most famous essays to making a list of specific national characteristics in answer to Crèvecœur's famous question, "What then is the American, this new man?" Samuel E. Morison, when writing his *Oxford History*, did not hesitate to undertake a description of the American character at various stages of our history, even though he found it "so complex . . . that the excess of one quality was balanced by the excess of its reverse." James Truslow Adams wrote an entire book, *The American*, "to find out . . . the difference between the *real* and the merely *legal* American," for he felt no doubt that the American "*is* different . . . from the citizen of any other nation." But perhaps the most conclusive illustration is Turner's classic essay, "The Significance of the Frontier in American History." It is sometimes forgotten that the primary purpose of that essay was to explain the differentiation of the American from the European and to show why certain traits were dominant in the American strain.

Even among historians who have been more cautious in making explicit use of the concept of national character, extended study is given to American attitudes or beliefs which could hardly be supposed to exist in a distinctive form unless they were associated with a distinctive personality or character. Thus, Charles and Mary Beard have generalized about the American spirit and about American civilization; Vernon Parrington, Ralph H. Gabriel, and Merle Curti about American thought; Albert Bushnell Hart about American ideals; Louis M. Hacker and Louis B. Wright about the American tradition; Denis W. Brogan about the American character; and various writers about the American mind. That a typical national spirit or thought or tradition or mind or set of ideals could have developed without the development of a typical national character is at least doubtful.

The concept of national character, then, ranks as a major historical assumption and one which has colored the writing of a vast body of historical literature. It might be supposed that, in the case of such a basic concept, far-reaching attention would have been given to the rationale of the subject and that the idea would have been defined and elaborated with rigor and precision. Yet the fact is that historians have done very little either to clarify or to validate this concept which they employ so freely. The looseness with which the term "national character" is used and the inconsistent meanings which attach to it are striking evidence of the lack of adequate analysis. Because of these deficiencies, and especially because of the way in which the idea of national character got mixed up with doctrines of race, the entire concept has been called into very serious question, and it will be necessary, at a later point in this discussion, to examine this philosophical rejection of the concept. First, however, the inadequacies, the abuses, and the confusion in the use of the concept by historians need to be scrutinized.

The most basic ambiguity of all is that historians vary widely in their notion as to what constitutes national character. To some writers it implies an absolute quality, persisting without change from one generation to another and manifesting itself universally in all the individuals who compose the national group. To others it is little more than a statistical tendency for the individuals in one country at a particular time to evince a given trait in higher proportion than the individuals of some other country. This approach is essentially relativistic, and it contrasts with the absolute approach both in regarding national traits as changing responses to changing conditions and in regarding national character as something which may be found in a large enough proportion of the people (and which exists as national character, pragmatically, only because it is found in them) rather than as something which inheres in all the people (and is found in them, mystically, because it is the national character).

Despite the insight which Hippocrates and Herodotus had originally shown in recognizing that, if conditions determine character, character will change with conditions, it was unfortunately true that many later historical writers seemed to accept the absolute view, which ultimately found its most extreme expression in the early nineteenth century. Today it can no longer be taken seriously in its literal form, and we can only smile at such manifestations as Herder's assertion that the Teutonic vocal apparatus was naturally formed for the enunciation of German speech and that it would be a perversion for the Teutonic larynx to dally with any other language. But, in a more subtle form, the concept of a character which is shared in common by all the people still commands impressive support. For instance, Otto Bauer has argued that national character is far more than a mere similarity of traits in diverse individuals and that it is, rather, a "community of character." Community of character, he contended, does not imply that individuals of the same nation will be similar to one another but that "the same force has acted on the character of each individual. . . . While . . . similarity of character can only be observed in the majority of the members of the nation, the community of character, the fact that they all are the products of one and the same effective force, is common to all of them without exception."[4]

Many other writers whose view is far less carefully refined

4. Karl W. Deutsch, *Nationalism and Social Communication* (Boston: Technology Press of Massachusetts Institute of Technology; New York: John Wiley & Sons, 1953), p. 6, quotes this passage from Bauer, *Die Nationalitätenfrage und die Sozialdemokratie* (2d ed.; Vienna: Brand, 1924), pp. 124–25.

than Bauer's have held to the absolute point of view by setting up what Weber would have called "ideal typical" images to personify the character of given nations and then evaluating individual citizens according to the extent to which they correspond to these types. Thus John Bull remains the "typical Englishman," and the old-fashioned Yankee remains the "typical American" for many writers, despite the fact that the vast majority in the English and the American population do not now conform to these types, if, indeed, they ever did. In this case, there is no longer a mystical assertion that all Englishmen or all Americans are alike, but there is still an arbitrary assumption that specific qualities are peculiarly British or American and that the extent to which an individual is truly British or American depends upon the extent to which he possesses these qualities.

Against these fixed notions of national character, the few critics who concern themselves with the subject have made such headway as they can. Writers like Hans Kohn and Carlton J. H. Hayes have shown clearly that traits which are deemed most intrinsic to the "character" of a nation will change markedly and rapidly as historical circumstances change.[5] Thus at the beginning of the eighteenth century the English were considered volatile and unstable in political affairs, while the French seemed steady and even phlegmatic by comparison. But a century later these conceptions had been reversed, and it was the French who were regarded as political weathercocks. Other writers have accepted the idea that traits of national character are essentially tendencies which ebb and flow with the waxing and waning of historical forces. For instance, Frederick Jackson Turner conceived of American traits as developing under the impact of frontier forces, and he spoke with foreboding of what would happen to these traits when the frontier no longer existed to perpetuate them.

But, though many historians have adopted these more tenable

5. Carlton J. H. Hayes, *Essays on Nationalism* (New York: Macmillan Co., 1928); Hans Kohn, *The Idea of Nationalism* (New York: Macmillan Co., 1948). See especially the first chapter in each of these volumes.

concepts of what constitutes national character, most of them have done so implicitly, without much discussion of their premises, and the fact remains that there is no agreement, no uniform understanding, within the profession, as to what is meant by "national character" or as to what elements go to make it up.

Not only have historians failed to agree on what they mean by "national character"; they have also failed to agree on what kind of qualities should be taken into account as composing it. There is a vast difference between mere traits of behavior, such as writing from left to right or eating with a fork, which a given people may have in common, and traits of character, in which a deeply intrenched system of values is involved. It is to this difference that David Riesman alludes when he says that "cultural differences, no matter how forcefully they may strike the ear, the eye, or the nose, are not necessarily correlated with character differences of equal significance."[6] It would be a difficult task to draw a hard-and-fast theoretical distinction between cultural traits and character traits, for when modes of behavior are continued over a long period, society tends to attribute value to them, and where values are involved, character is involved, for character might almost be defined as the individual's system or complex of values. Erich Fromm has stated this relationship between behavior and character with remarkable clarity, as follows: "In order that any society may function well, its members must acquire the kind of character which makes them *want* to act in the way they *have* to act as members of the society or of a special class within it. They have to *desire* what objectively is *necessary* for them to do. *Outer force* is to be replaced by *inner compulsion* and by the particular kind of human energy which is channeled into character traits."[7]

6. "Psychological Types and National Character," *American Quarterly*, V (1953), 330.

7. "Individual and Social Origins of Neurosis," in Clyde Kluckhohn and Henry A. Murray (eds.), *Personality in Nature, Society, and Culture* (New York: Alfred A. Knopf, 1949), p. 409.

But, though no one can be expected to make a rigorous distinction between traits of behavior and traits of character, it is easy to see that if we follow Fromm in regarding character as a force exercising inner compulsion, we must reject large segments of the data which historians have used in describing national character. For they have often lumped together indiscriminately the basic traits which play a dynamic part in shaping character and the mere extraneous practices which serve as visible recognition signs by which the underlying character traits may be perceived. Very often a catalogue of traits ranges from the profound to the trivial. Thus we may be told in the same breath that Americans are optimistic (a trait of temperament), that they attach great value to productive activity (a trait of character), that they are fond of jazz music (a cultural trait), and that they are remarkably prone to join organized groups (a behavioral trait which may provide overt evidence of some underlying trait of character). In the discussion of national character it probably would not be either practicable or rewarding to enforce these distinctions rigidly, but analysis of the subject would not be quite so loose as it is if writers had at least recognized that traits of character are at one level and distinctive habits, such as addiction to some particular article of diet, are at quite another.

Along with this somewhat indiscriminate lumping together of various kinds of traits, there has been a practice also of examining separate traits in a piecemeal fashion, without recognition of the fact that character, if it exists at all, is a complex or a Gestalt which must be examined and understood in its totality. I know no better illustration of the problem which arises here than a statement by Charles R. Buxton, comparing a series of different nationalities. Carlton J. H. Hayes cited this passage as an example of oversimple categorizing of national types, which it certainly is, but it is also a striking example of the way in which particularly conspicuous traits may be torn out of the context of character of which they are part and displayed as a kind of cabinet of curiosities. "Just as England contributes her sense for political liberty," said Buxton, "France her intellectual honesty and lucidity, Germany her industry and discipline, Italy her aesthetic aptitude, so Finland has her advanced democracy, Poland her music and art, Bohemia religious independence, the Serbs their warm poetic temperament, the Greeks their subtlety and their passion for the past, the Bulgarians their plodding endurance and taciturn energy, the Armenians their passion for education and progress."

Waiving the very big question whether these generalizations have any validity in the first place, the point is that the traits mentioned do not recognize the whole of character but simply seize upon certain fragments or aspects or manifestations of character. Impulses toward political liberty on the part of the English or toward discipline on the part of the Germans are part of a characterological adjustment to voluntaristic or authoritarian systems of human relationships which find expression not only in political life but also in family organization, the economic order, the intellectual orbit, and elsewhere. Similarly, the "lucidity" of the French or the "warm poetic temperament" of the Serbs do not mean anything, unless they mean that one society has experienced conditions which fostered a rationalistic and pragmatic adjustment to life, while the other has developed amid circumstances which were conducive to imaginative and emotional responses. In the next chapter I shall have more to say about this problem of recognizing character in its totality, but, for the present, perhaps these illustrations will suffice to show how badly the true analysis of national character will be hindered if historians, like the blind men who examined the elephant, mistake the part for the whole.

Confusions of a different kind have arisen from the fact that writers on national character have neglected to give adequate attention to the nature of the unit within which the alleged character may be said to exist. This difficulty begins with the fact that, in the political sense, a nation is, of course, simply a governmental unit, having jurisdiction over the people within a recognized area. As such, it could not possibly determine the characteristics of a people, which are determined socially, economically, or culturally rather than politically. Hence it might be argued that group character is never national character in any strict sense, since the unit within which group character develops is the distinctive culture or the unique civilization rather than the nation. In point of pure logic, this argument would, in fact, be entirely valid; but the character of a culture may become, or at least coincide with, the character of a nation, because the culture tends to realize itself politically through the process of national unification. When the culture has fulfilled the demands of its own nature by expressing itself in this way, the culture group becomes for all practical purposes a national group, and the cultural character becomes also the national character. That is, if a French national character exists, it is not because common citizenship or common residence in France made the French people alike but because the French people were alike and, being alike, achieved a national framework for their culture, so that their character has its setting within this frame. The degree of distinctiveness of the national character, therefore, will always depend upon the extent to which the nation uniquely embodies a unique culture. For instance, the Scandinavian culture has found embodiment not in one nation but in three, and it cannot be expected that the national characters of Norway, Sweden, and Denmark will be very sharply differentiated. Similarly, it has been argued that Canada and the United States are mere political divisions of "what is practically a single nationality" (i.e., culture).[8] On the other hand, where a unique culture has expressed itself in a single nation, as in the case of Japan, a highly distinctive national character may be found.

8. Deutsch, *op. cit.*, p. 218, n. 37, quoting statement by Henry Pratt Fairchild in *Dictionary of Sociology* (New York: Philosophical Library, Inc., 1944), p. 201.

This tendency for the culture to fulfil itself politically as a nation, and therefore for the culture and the nation to coincide, serves to reduce somewhat the difficulty of defining the unit within which national character may be thought to exist. But it by no means disposes of the difficulty altogether, for the whole problem of nationality is far too complex to admit of any easy solutions. For instance, we frequently encounter the statement that one of the bonds which unifies a people is their residence together in a common territory. This view, however, is based upon a circular argument, for the test of the nation is the existence of the common territory, and the test of whether the territory is common is its position within national limits. As Karl W. Deutsch has cogently pointed out, we think of New York and San Francisco as being part of a common territory but of New York and Montreal or Detroit and Toronto as lacking this bond. If geographical similarity and contiguity cannot provide "common territory" for two communities, while political jurisdiction can, the concept of "common territory" clearly begs the question.[9]

At another level, one finds the argument that common historical experience provides the bonds of nationality. John Stuart Mill expressed this view when he said that "the strongest cause for the feeling of nationality . . . is identity of political antecedents; the possession of a national history, and consequent community of recollections; collective pride and humiliation, pleasure and regret, connected with the same incidents in the past." But, to cite Deutsch again, this explanation of the basis of national unity runs afoul of the question, "Just when or how has 'one and the same force' of history been experienced by that majority of the American people whose ancestors immigrated to the United States *after* the American Revolution?"[10]

At the conclusion of a brilliant analysis, Deutsch declares, "It

9. Deutsch, *op. cit.*, p. 4.
10. *Ibid.*, pp. 5–6, including quotation from Mill, *Representative Government.*

is now clear why all the usual descriptions of a people in terms of a community of languages, of character, or memories, or past history, are open to exception. For what counts is not the presence or absence of any single factor, but merely the presence of sufficient communication facilities with enough complementarity to produce the overall result. . . . What is proposed here, in short, is a functional definition of nationality. Membership in a people essentially consists in wide complementarity of social communication. It consists in the ability to communicate more effectively, and over a wider range of subjects, with members of one large group than with outsiders."[11]

Cogent and illuminating as this statement is, it still leaves the student of national character with a highly difficult problem, for his is the responsibility for discovering by the exercise of intensive research and careful judgment just where the boundaries of "complementarity of social communication" lie in the case of any given group. Until he has thus translated theory into findings, he still cannot do more than guess where the limits of any one national character are fixed or whether given character groups are objective realities or mere figments of a chauvinistic imagination.

The whole subject of nationalism is so full of complexity that the problem of the historian, or any other investigator, would be difficult enough if the national group were the only group which he needed to take into account. It would be task enough for him to have to determine whether a given population can be objectively identified as a nationality group and, if it can, what degree of distinctiveness sets it apart from other nationality groups. But in reality he can never isolate his factors in this way, and he must constantly reckon with the fact that the members of his nationality group are also and simultaneously members of occupational groups, religious groups, or social classes, and the character traits which he discovers in them are not necessarily

11. *Op. cit.*, p. 71.

traits of national character but may be occupational or religious or class traits. Thus he is confronted by the problem of distinguishing between traits which are attributable to the nationality and those which are attributable to membership in some other group. In a society such as ours, with its multiplicity of overlapping social groups, this is a highly treacherous source of confusion, especially since the members of a single nationality group often tend to show a very high proportion of membership in some one religious group or occupational group or class group, and the qualities of these latter groups thus bear a specious appearance of belonging to the nationality group as such. For instance, if the inhabitants of Scotland are dour, it may be as much because they are Calvinists as because they are Scots; if the compatriots of Thomas Jefferson were self-reliant and individualistic, it was perhaps as much because they were landowning, subsistence farmers as because they were Americans; and if a subject of Queen Victoria was cold toward strangers, it may have been because, as a member of a class-conscious society, he was appalled at the thought of behaving familiarly toward someone outside his own class, rather than because he was English.

At first glance, the distinctions here may seem academic or even false. If the English were class-conscious and the Scots were Calvinistic, do not the qualities of class-consciousness and of Calvinism then become English traits and Scottish traits? However plausible this assumption may seem, the fact is that the twain do not become one, and two serious forms of confusion will arise when they are treated as one. In the first place, although the two groups may appear to coincide, the coincidence never attains completeness. Many of the Highland Scots are Catholics, and many of the English today are no longer conditioned to the class standards of Victoria's time. These individuals, too, must be taken into account. In the second place, great errors will result if the qualities which derive from or are attributable to one social condition are disassociated from that condition and attributed by the student to some second condition with which the first may coincide. For, in such cases, the problem of causality is always involved, and fallacies are certain to follow if one treats class traits or religious traits as if they were national traits and then seeks explanations for them in national terms.

Although a given population may be identified with two groups (religious and national, religious and occupational, or what not) and thus the two groupings may coincide in the same population, the fact remains that the forces which operate to produce these groupings do not coincide. Consequently, serious confusion in analysis can result from treating the traits found in the population as if they were interchangeably attributable to either one of these forces. The nature of this confusion might be illustrated by considering, for instance, the people of Sweden, who are predominantly blond and are also Lutheran almost to a man. Yet no one would assert that blondness is a quality of Lutheranism or, for that matter, that Lutheranism is characteristic of blonds. In this particular case the convergence in one group (the Swedes) of attributes from diverse bodies (an ethnic strain and a religious denomination), to both of which the members of the group belong, causes no confusion, and the attempt to link them is patently ridiculous. But in other situations it is almost impossible to avoid confusion. For instance, Americans are said to be competitive, materialistic, and comfort-loving. It is also known that America has a middle-class population proportionately far greater than the middle class of any other country. When we observe competitive or materialistic or comfort-loving manifestations in this country, to what extent are we witnesses of characteristically American traits, to what extent of middle-class traits fortuitously displayed in America?

Long experience has repeatedly shown that a traveler visiting the United States and meeting, let us say, a property-owning, Methodist electrician, age twenty-five, is likely to explain all the traits of the individual, whether deriving from his occupation, his religion, his economic status, or even his youth and his sex, as attributes of his Americanism. This is to be expected. But when the historian or the social analyst draws upon the traveler's report, a discrimination between the various factors becomes his responsibility. By and large, the responsibility has not been met, and many historians writing on national character have not refined very much beyond the traveler.

The problem involved here is not merely a matter of deciding what traits should be interpreted as traits of nationality; it is also one of evaluating the relative importance of alternative classificatory groupings for purposes of social analysis. Has modern nationalism caused us to exaggerate the importance of national character and to minimize the importance of the traits which are attributable to social class? Is it the fact that they are Americans, or the fact that they are predominantly middle class, which does most to explain the people of the United States? On the one hand, David Riesman aptly observes that "it is often said that a burger of Lyons is closer in type to a burger of Bremen or Buffalo than any of them is to a factory worker in his own country";[12] and Hans Kohn remarks that "the character of an occupational group, such as peasants, soldiers, civil servants, may be as clearly defined and stable as any character of a national group, or even more so";[13] on the other hand, Karl Deutsch warns against too narrow an application of the occupational concept: "Efficient communication among engineers, artists, or stamp collectors is limited to a relatively narrow segment of their total range of activities. In most other things they do, in their childhood memories, in courtship, marriage, and parenthood, in their standards of beauty, their habits of food and drink, in games and recreation, they are far closer to mutual communication and understanding with their countrymen than with their fellow specialists in other countries."[14]

12. *Op. cit.*, p. 328.
13. *Op. cit.*, p. 11.
14. *Op. cit.*, p. 72.

Deutsch goes on to suggest that, where the cleavages of social class are very deep, they may become more important than common nationality and that they may even justify Disraeli's idea of "the two nations . . . the rich and the poor." The point, however, is not that one concept is valid and the other fallacious but that the student of history or of society must recognize that in some cases national character is far more uniform and distinctive than in others, and that the degree to which he relies upon the concept must be in proportion to the degree to which national character actually constitutes a valid and useful means of generalization. Always the national-character concept should be held in balance against other group-character concepts which may illuminate the study of people.

On the whole, historians have been extremely casual in their approach to all these problems, and their use of the concept of national character has suffered accordingly. It would hardly be too strong an indictment to say that many of them have written freely about the "national character" of the people of a given country without ever determining for themselves or indicating for the reader what they conceive the nature of "national character" to be, what components in a people's personality and behavior they regard as constituting "character"; what relationship they suppose to exist between a specific trait and the character as a totality; how they would define or delimit the "nation" as the unit to which the character is attributed; how they would distinguish the "national" characteristics from class characteristics, religious characteristics, or other group characteristics in a given aggregation of people; and, finally, how they would determine the relative importance of national character in comparison with other forms of group character as keys for the interpretation of a society.

Such an indictment, with charges of imprecision, looseness, and vagueness, might have been drawn. But it was not drawn, and, for the most part, use of the concept of national character did not incur criticism on these grounds. But there was still another aspect of the problem with which historians failed to deal adequately: this was their analysis of the determinants or causative factors in national character. On this phase of the problem their shortcomings have incurred heavy criticism and have even led to a reaction against using the concept at all.

Until quite recent years, almost all attempts to account for the existence of national character have resorted to one of three accepted forms of explanation. The earliest of these was the supernatural argument that God had designated the given group as a chosen people and had endowed them with the superior qualities that were pleasing in his eyes. This claim is commonly associated with the Jews, but, in fact, it has been put forward in more or less formalized manner by any number of other national groups. In America it was clearly indicated in the first large-scale history of the country—George Bancroft's famous work—and it had been suggested as early as 1668 in Massachusetts, when the Reverend William Stoughton declared that God "had sifted a whole nation that he might send choice grain [the colonists] over into this Wilderness."

A second form of explanation stressed the determinative force of environmental factors. Fundamentally, this line of reasoning was stronger than any other, for it depended essentially upon the proposition that people will be influenced by the circumstances and conditions in which they live and that collective responses to distinctive conditions will in time take the form of collective traits that are themselves distinctive. If this approach had been followed up by trained men who were aware of the complexities of social analysis, a science of national character might have emerged many decades ago, but, in fact, the application of the environmental premise fell into the hands of amateurs who formulated it so crudely and worked it out so poorly that, in the long run, they seriously compromised their own point of view.

Max Hildebert Boehm, discussing national character in the *Encyclopaedia of the Social Sciences*, observes that the most prolific writers on this subject include "scientific travelers, historians, poets, members of military expeditions, and tourists," all more than ready to comment on the peoples of the countries which they visited. The list is, I think, a revealing one, for it is made up of amateurs—poets and tourists—giving rein to their intuitions, and experts on other subjects—botanists on expedition, generals on campaign—handling the question of national character with their left hands. As descriptive writers, they at least possessed the qualification of having observed the peoples whom they described, but for explaining what they saw they often had no qualifications whatever. Hence environmental explanation was oversimplified almost invariably and was often fantastic. Baron Montesquieu, for instance, seized upon the climate and attempted to explain English love of liberty as resulting from the cold and dampness of England. Another writer argued that English humidity prevents people from seeing objects in very sharp outline, thus hinders the activity of the imagination, and consequently impels the Englishman to become a man of deeds rather than of ideas. This is hardly more scientific than Oscar Wilde's speculation as to whether the fogs caused the English mentality or the English mentality caused the fogs.

Other writers of a romantic disposition have sought to explain character in terms of landscape—attributing the aloof pride and stark gravity of the Spaniards, for instance, to the forbidding bleakness and harshness of the Spanish terrain.

These absurd examples are in a sense unfair to the environmentalists, and one must instantly concede that the climatologists, geographers, physiographers, and similar experts have made invaluable contributions in showing how physical circumstances may condition the traits of a group. In this connection it is only necessary to remember that Frederick Jackson Turner's frontier hypothesis is an environmental explanation of Americanism, and

I suppose that very few analysts, even including his critics, would deny that what Turner offered is, thus far, the most important single insight into the American character. Yet it remains true that attempts to apply the environmental approach thoroughly and analytically have been rare and that, on the whole, environmentalists disregarded several factors which required full consideration in any proper formulation of the theory of national character.

One of these mistakes has been the tendency of environmentalists to dwell upon the primary or physical environment and upon such factors in it as geography, climate, and natural resources, to the neglect of man-made conditions that surround us. Anthropologists have exposed the fallacy of this approach by pointing out that man creates a secondary environment—the environment of the city, the environment of modern technology—which is in its origin cultural but in its completed form as purely physical as the weather or the terrain. This secondary environment has increasingly influenced the lives of men, at the expense of the primary or natural environment. For instance, the induced fertility of an irrigated tract becomes more important culturally than the natural aridity of the region. In North America the effective environment of the aboriginal Indians was, for all practical purposes, entirely different from that of the American people today, though the primary environment was the same. Far more recently than the Indians, our grandfathers lived in an environment which contrasts sharply with our own: theirs, for instance, offered them economic occupation as subsistence farmers, working separately, responsible only to themselves, and accommodating their routine to the rhythm of the seasons; ours offers us occupation primarily as paid employees, working in groups, under direction, and with a routine controlled by the clock. Such circumstances may well condition the traits of large numbers of people, but factors of this kind seldom receive due consideration when the determinants of national character are being weighed.

Another deficiency, even more basic, is that, while the various branches of social study have for a long time past given careful attention to the forces which operate upon man, they made but little effort until recently to understand man as the object upon which these forces operated. It would seem, offhand, that in any consideration of the influence of an environmental factor upon the character of a group of people, two things are imperatively necessary: knowledge of the operation of the factor and knowledge of the human receptor upon which the factor impinges. Yet, as I have remarked in the Introduction, the nature of the society upon which environmental forces play has often been ignored by historians. They discuss the impact of natural wealth upon men as if any random group of human beings would have responded similarly to the same force, without recognition of the fact that only a society with a certain technology is capable of responding. They speculate upon the effect of war on national morals, without knowing, in fact, by what process or at what age moral values are formed. They are sure, therefore, that the "lost generation" became lost because of war, bootleg liquor, or jazz music, and they blandly ignore the fact that if current emphases upon the long-range effects of infant nurture are correct, then Scott Fitzgerald and his contemporaries must have become lost sometime early in the Edwardian era.

But it was not the careless use of the environmental approach which finally brought the national-character concept to a crisis. The difficulties in applying the environmental factor, and all the other difficulties that have been mentioned here, were problems from which history might ultimately have contrived to extricate itself. They were, one might say, the normal problems, perhaps somewhat greater in degree, which always arise in the course of any study of society. But during the nineteenth century the mild process of academic inquiry about national character as an aspect of generalization concerning social groups was caught in the backwash of modern nationalism, with its overpowering drive to erect a myth of distinctive national virtues flourishing within a framework of completely separate national identity. From this time forward, the confusions surrounding the subject were no longer the consequences of mere scholarly imprecision. They were, rather, results of the collision between two ideas of national character, motivated by two entirely different purposes. One was the rational but relatively defenseless idea of a tendency toward similarity among people who live under similar conditions and in association with one another. The other was the mystic idea of an entire people supernaturally bound together by the common heritage of a national soul—an idea propelled by the overwhelming force of modern nationalism.

The spokesmen of nationalism brought into prominence the third form of causative explanation, namely, the "genetic" or "racial" argument. Here was a line of reasoning with immense appeal to unscientific minds: if physical traits, such as skin pigment, are transmitted by heredity, then character traits must also be transmitted in this way. So ran the argument, and no idea could have been more congenial to the ethnocentric impulses which exist in almost every society. When these impulses were harnessed to extreme and malignant forms of nationalism, they were immensely accentuated, and national historians writing under the influence of this new force found a perfect device for national glorification in the argument that a superior national character had been transmitted in the blood stream from superior forebears in the past. This superiority, being congenital, was also exclusive, and lesser folk, no matter how great their good will, could not share in it. A vast pseudo-scientific façade was erected by writers like Count Gobineau, who formulated the Nordic myth in his *Essay on the Inequality of Human Races* in 1855.

From that time until the fall of Hitler, a whole battalion of writers was constantly ready to contend, *pari passu*, that racial inheritance proved the existence of national traits and that national traits proved the validity of racist doctrine. We have nothing to gain by the examination of these notions in detail. Suffice it to say that while they flourished they seemed inseparably linked with the idea of national character, and as they were discredited some of the stigma which attached to them came to be associated also with the national-character idea. Thus the way was paved for a sharp reaction against the whole concept of national character.

There had long been a latent basis for such a reaction, in the doubt entertained by men of discriminating mind, like John Stuart Mill, who had declared in 1849 that "of all vulgar modes of escaping from the consideration of the effect of social and moral influences on the human mind, the most vulgar is that of attributing diversities of character to inherent natural differences." But the reaction itself apparently began to develop shortly before or during the 1930's. In 1933, Boehm, writing authoritatively on the then current status of the concept of national character, declared that "during . . . the nineteenth century, . . . the idea of the character of an epoch came to displace that of national character," and while we may doubt that the racists were effectively challenged as early as he indicates, we may well infer that the concept was no longer in high repute at the time when he wrote. In 1936, Rudolph Rocker, in his brilliant attack on modern nationalism, entitled *Nationalism and Culture* (English trans.; New York: Covici, Friede, 1937), spoke of the deep cleavages between various groups within a "nation" and asserted that "the differences of economic interest and intellectual effort within the nation have naturally developed special habits and modes of living among the members of the various social classes. It is, therefore, very venturesome to speak of a community of national customs and morals" (p. 270). In 1940, Hamilton Fyfe published a book entitled *The Illusion of National Character*, in which he vigorously assailed the racists and asserted that "there are no 'national character types' . . . never have been typical English or Americans, French or Germans." Despite Fyfe's dogmatic title and his sweeping assertions, a careful reading of his book will show that what he rejected was not the idea of national character as such but the concept of an unalterable, genetically determined national character—not the proposition that the majority of a national population may collectively tend to acquire certain adaptive traits but the idea that all the members of a national population are destined to possess certain inherent traits.[15] He was, in fact, repudiating racism rather than national character, but in his indignation he treated the two as identical and, in effect, threw the baby out with the bath. His reaction provides a striking illustration of the injury which the racist rationale has done to the concept of national character.

So far as I know, no one came forward to challenge Fyfe, and the growth of Nazi power made clear to everyone the vicious implications inherent in racist doctrine. Many people must have felt as did W. H. Auden: "I can't believe that the character of one nation is much different from that of another." In 1944, Frederick Hertz said, "We may speak of a national character by analogy only, as we also speak of the character of a landscape which comprises many different things, and still forms a certain unity to the eye of the geologist, botanist, zoologist, geographer, or artist."[16]

15. Note the generalizations about group character in this passage, which denies the existence of any Dutch national character on the ground that the Dutch in Holland and the Dutch in South Africa are dissimilar:

"The Dutch in South Africa have nothing in common with the Dutch in Holland. They took with them from their native land a tradition of intense cleanliness, of household neatness and order. Settling in a country where water is scarce, they could not be continually washing either themselves or the floors. On their long waggon-treks, in search of soil to settle on, they lost also the house-pride that is so strong in Holland. The liking for society, natural to the inhabitants of a small, thickly-populated State, the Boers exchanged for that love of solitude which is usually found in people who live in an undeveloped empty country at a great distance from one another. If they could see on the horizon another farmer's smoke, they complained of overcrowding! Put in a position which enabled them to treat the natives as they pleased, many of them became brutal to a degree which was utterly foreign to, and which painfully shocked, the kindly people of Holland" (*The Illusion of National Character* [London: Watts & Co., 1940; rev. ed., 1947], p. 24).

16. *Nationality in History and Politics* (London: Kegan Paul, Ltd., 1944), p. 41.

As recently as 1952, Boyd C. Shafer, writing in the *American Historical Review* under the significant title "Men Are More Alike," has said, "Nor is there any such thing as a constant or ever-present national character, unless it is invented by historians." Shafer quotes Sir John Seeley as saying that "no explanation is so vague, so cheap, and so difficult to verify."

Almost all recent discussion which examined national character in methodological terms has questioned the idea or denied its validity altogether. The reaction against it has made a wide swing, and today the concept is under a serious cloud, if not entirely discredited.

This repudiation of national character as a philosophical concept has left historians in a paradoxical situation, for, as I have already shown, they continue to utilize the concept for operational purposes even when they fail to defend it as an idea. It meets with almost universal skepticism when scrutinized as a concept, and it enjoys almost universal adoption at the pragmatic level. The field of historical method, therefore, scarcely presents any problems more conspicuous than the questions why historians build so much of their writing upon a concept to which they will not give philosophical indorsement and whether there is any means by which they can justify their use of this seemingly questionable idea.

At first glance one might suppose that this continued adherence to the concept is simply an aspect of the historian's addiction to the theme of "national glory." But, in fact, generalizations about national character are heavily used by many historians who write with almost clinical detachment and without any hyperpatriotic impulses whatever. If we are to find a motivation which will explain the continued use of the concept by historians who are now active, we must seek something less obvious than patriotism. We must look not so much to the bias of the writer as to the compulsions of the medium, and we must remember that, when human history is broken down into a series of histories of separate nations, this manner of organizing the subject will create certain necessities in the treatment of the material, whether the nation is viewed with chauvinistic pride or with Olympian objectivity and aloofness. Specifically, it will require the historian, as a writer, to show, as every writer must, that the unit about which he writes is a real unit, possessing objective existence outside his own conceptual plan, and that it is not an artificial or imaginary unit. This compulsion must control him far more basically than any patriotic impulse; for national history may or may not have a theme of glory, but it must have a theme of some kind, and it cannot have a theme at all unless its subject has unity.

In establishing the unity of his subject, the national historian today cannot rely, as his nineteenth-century predecessor might have done, upon the political unity of the nation. So long as the historian regarded history as "past politics," he could always focus upon such political manifestations as the state, its constitution, its rulers, and its policy. But today a new historical emphasis insists that the historian must give full consideration to social and cultural developments. When he broadens his history in this way to include the total experience of a people, no unifying theme remains unless the people themselves are collectively distinguishable from other peoples. Study of the American people holds little intellectual attraction if the American people are merely an undifferentiated mass of humans fortuitously located in America, but it takes on more positive value if Americans can be regarded as possessing distinctive traits and social adaptations which characterize them as a group. Similarly, the history of American events would be devoid of intellectual challenge if it were merely a literal recording of any events that chanced to occur within American territorial limits. The purpose of history is not simply to show that events which might have happened to anyone did happen to someone, but rather to explain why a special sequence of events befell a particular aggregation of people. To do this, history must find, as a unifying factor, what is distinctive in the circumstances, the condition, and the experience of the aggregation in question. But unique circumstances, conditions, and experience are apt to produce unique traits and attitudes among the people as a whole. To recognize such collective traits and attitudes, as historians are prone to do, is to embrace the concept of national character.

In so far as the compulsions of the medium cause historians to adopt this concept, it prevails not because of the strength of the theory on which it is founded but because of the historian's need for it as a unifying device or expedient. Art requires it, even if the data do not impose it, and the need for such a concept in historical synthesis is so great that, if it did not exist, it would, like Voltaire's God, have to be invented.

Thus the paradox deepens, for it would seem that one of the chief reasons which prompts the historian to use this concept is of a kind which cannot aid him in defending his use of it. The further one examines the subject, the more it appears that history has reached an impasse in its handling of national character. It has failed either to formulate in clear terms what is meant by "national character" or to develop a rationale by which the existence of such character can be validated. It has rejected "race" as a basis for explaining national character but has not worked out any adequate substitute basis to put in its place. Consequently, an increasing number of historians have rejected "national character" as an overt idea, though many of them have continued to put forward historical interpretations which were dependent upon it as an unstated and perhaps unconscious assumption. Those who defended it did so on impressionistic or intuitive grounds, and there is perhaps more meaning than was intended in Professor Commager's allusion to the "alchemy" by which national character is formed. The one thing which we can say with assurance about alchemy is that it is a pseudo-science.

Yet, despite this apparent repudiation, the cause, it would seem, is not altogether hopeless. The hypothesis that group similarities, with their reflections in the group character, may develop along national lines is essentially no less tenable than the now popular hypothesis that they may develop along class lines or occupational lines. The real problem of history is to separate academic and rational theories of national character from chauvinistic and mystical theories, and to do this rigorously and with finality. History itself has made but little progress in articulating a new and tenable theory of national character, and, particularly, it has failed to settle upon an adequate rationale to replace the discredited rationale of race. But, meanwhile, it now appears that, in new quarters, the existence of national character is being reaffirmed on sounder and more analytical grounds.[17] A more factual demonstration of the reality of national character and a more scientific approach to the concept are being worked out, and, though the grounds on which it is defended are controversial, they are far more tenable than any in the past. The exponents of this new interpretation are primarily the behavioral scientists—anthropologists engaged in the analysis of culture, sociologists engaged in analyzing the social system, and social psychologists interested in personality. The fields of study of these specialists lie outside my professional competence, yet their analyses of the traits of national character are so pertinent to the work of the historian that he must seek to understand them. For this reason I shall attempt in the next chapter to show how the behavioral scientists have dealt with some of the problems which history has failed to solve, and I shall also examine three important studies of the American character by behavioral scientists. In this examination I shall proceed with the double purpose of seeing what history may derive from the methods of the behavioral scientists and of showing wherein history may strengthen certain weak points that the behavioral sciences have not been able to correct.

17. See Margaret Mead, "The Study of National Character," in Daniel Lerner (ed.), *The Policy Sciences: Recent Developments in Scope and Method* (Stanford, Calif.: Stanford University Press, 1951), pp. 70–85; Otto Klineberg, "A Science of National Character," *Journal of Social Psychology,* XIX (1944), 147–62.

II. The Behavioral
Scientists and National Character

If a historian of diplomacy were to review the attitude of his col-
leagues in the American field toward the concept of national
character, he might observe that they accord it a *de facto* but not
a *de jure* status. They are fluent in allusions to the American mind,
the American spirit, the American creed, the American tradition,
and so on, and they often employ the theme of American character as a unifying device. Indeed, the rationale of treating American history as distinguishable from any other history depends
upon regarding the American people as distinguishable. But since
the repudiation of the doctrine of race characteristics historians
have handled the *explanation*, as opposed to the *description*, of national character in a gingerly fashion. Mark Twain once made a
remark to the effect that a cat which has once sat on a hot stove
lid will never sit on another, but it will not sit on a cold one
either. For the cats of the historical profession, the stove lid was
the causal analysis of national character, and it had been heated
red-hot with racism. It burned so badly that the cats now experience marked professional discomfort in approaching the stove lid
at all, and they prefer to remain at a safe distance, where they can
merely describe character without explaining it. When the historian treats the people of a selected area, such as the United States,
as a homogeneous unit, he usually assumes this unity as given and
makes no effort to defend the validity of his unit in the way that
would be expected, for instance, of a zoölogist when treating the
fauna of a selected area. Thus, as I suggested at the conclusion of
the preceding chapter, it has fallen to investigators in other, non-
historical branches of learning to undertake a more searching and
more systematic analysis of national character and its determinants.

The essential weakness that has always disabled historians in their effort to deal with the subject scientifically has been their failure to recognize that national character is not a separate phenomenon in itself but simply one specialized manifestation of group character. Group character in turn is but a composite of individual characters, and individual character is simply a pattern in that complex of human processes and qualities which are designated nowadays by the term "personality." The study of national character, therefore, is properly a branch of the study of group character and of personality. Only when it is recognized as such can it make real advances.

These fields of inquiry, with which the study of national character must be linked, were scarcely recognized as legitimate areas of study until the past few decades. During the nineteenth century, it is true, there was a subject known as "psychology," which dealt with the curiosities of individual conduct, and another, known as "anthropology," which dealt with the curiosities of group conduct, especially among exotic and primitive peoples. But no one conceived that the many facets of individual conduct might be scrutinized as the overt aspect of a single personality which could be understood only in an integral sense, as a totality, and no one conceived that the many facets of group conduct might be understood as the overt aspect of a single culture which also could be understood only in an integral sense, as a totality.

At least these things were not understood prior to the work of Sigmund Freud. Freud recognized that the workings of the personality could be understood only by piercing through the superficial zones of intellect and reason to the vasty, irrational deeps of the id and the ego beneath. He saw almost all psychopathic conduct as compensating for basic drives which had been thwarted. and he saw vast areas of thought, like folklore and religion, as great screens on which anxieties, wishes, and impulses were projected from the subconscious, but in such translated terms that their origin and meaning would be hidden. All these concepts contributed to an integral view of the personality, and, though it may seem an anticlimactic thing to say about a man around whom such fierce conflict has raged, perhaps Freud's greatest contribution was in viewing the personality as an entirety.

Freud himself conducted all his intensive analyses among a limited number of individuals, all of whom were products of the civilization of western Europe. Finding certain universal reactions among these people, he rather naturally supposed that these reactions were common to all mankind and were biologically or physiologically conditioned. Thus he appealed fairly freely to the concept of "instinct," and he personally would probably have insisted upon the uniformity of men as human beings rather than upon their diversity as products of diverse cultures. But, though he relied very heavily upon biological explanations for phenomena, later students, while applying his basic methods, observed that human groups outside Western society did not always develop the reactions which he had regarded as universal. For instance, in some societies, adolescence was found to be an easy transition period and not a troubled time of crisis; in others, the Oedipus drive of a son to replace his father in the affections of his mother did not seem to appear. Finally, critics began to suspect that Freud's greatest weakness had been that he overemphasized "the biological origin of mental characteristics" and that, through assuming "that the instinctual drives . . . that are frequent in our culture are biologically determined," he had disregarded cultural factors and thus had blocked "an understanding of the real forces which motivate our attitudes and actions."[1] Thus a considerable modification of Freud began to set in, and such eminent figures as Erich Fromm and Karen Horney devoted much of their effort to retooling Freudian theory to take account of cultural forces that had conditioned the personality in various basic ways.

Once the psychologist takes this step, he stands on the verge

1. Karen Horney, *The Neurotic Personality of Our Time* (New York: W. W. Norton & Co., 1937), p. 20.

of accepting a concept of group character. In so far as the Oedipus complex or any other complex is peculiar to a certain culture, precisely to that extent do the people identified with this culture possess a group character, and once the concept of group character is adopted, the concept of national character as one particular variant or form of group character can hardly be denied. Thus, by a process unsuspected at the time, the development of Freudian theory and of psychoanalysis was beginning to provide a new rationale for the concept of national character.

Meanwhile, additional support for the concept was being generated in another unforeseen quarter—namely, in the field of anthropology. Here the critical step came when students of primitive man began to use the term "culture" in a new sense. Traditionally, "culture" had meant a collection of artifacts, actually or potentially on show in a museum. But in very recent decades, it has come to mean a collection of customs, a series of habits, though the change is so recent that it was not recorded either in the *New English Dictionary* or in the supplement which recorded usages as recent as 1928.

Inasmuch as a recent volume has been devoted exclusively to analyzing various possible definitions of "culture," I will not here make the mistake of attempting any one definition. Ralph Linton spoke of culture simply as "the way of life in any society," and, to point up the distinction between society and culture, he said, "Societies are organized groups of individuals, and cultures are, in the last analysis, nothing more than the organized repetitive responses of a society's members." On another occasion, he defined "culture" in two words as "social heredity." Still another of his expressions was the statement that "a consensus of behavior and opinion constitutes a culture pattern."

This concept of culture has given to the study of society the same integrating effect which the Freudian concept of personality has given to the study of the individual. If "the way of life," or "the organized repetitive responses," of a society are to be understood, they must be understood in a totality and not as a series of random and curious phenomena. Thus, as Kardiner has remarked, "when an ethnographer reports that in a given society divorces are frequent; that the accounts of religious dogmas and rituals are inaccurate and inconsistent; that when people are ill they just lie down and die; that they have little interest in permanent structures; that they have no conscience or tendency to depressive reactions—all these may be unrelated events, or may be deeply interconnected. It makes a great deal of difference, as far as the workings of society are concerned, which view we adopt. If these traits are interrelated, then they are only peripheral points which indicate how the social process [as a whole] is operating."[2]

The unifying effect of the culture concept as a means for viewing society as a totality was, perhaps, the first major value implicit in the concept. A second value of transcendent importance was the great effectiveness of the concept as an explanation of the determinative forces which operate upon the individual personality. Exponents of the cultural view have demonstrated very clearly that naked environmental forces do not operate directly and in gross form upon the human personality. If they did, all human beings would react similarly to the same external stimuli; but we know that this is a condition contrary to fact, partly because no individual is capable of reacting to more than a tiny fraction of the countless stimuli which the environment projects upon him and partly because nothing has been more thoroughly proved than the fact that differently conditioned people will respond to identical stimuli in different ways. Until the concept of culture was introduced, there was no adequate basis for explaining these diversities in reaction; but the concept provides a comprehensive basis of explanation, for it presents the culture as a screen or filter which bars out some of the conditions in the environment and prevents them from having any impact upon the personality or

2. *The Psychological Frontiers of Society* (New York: Columbia University Press, 1945), p. xviii.

even upon the consciousness, while it admits the stimuli of certain other conditions and even amplifies their strength as stimuli. Clyde Kluckhohn and Henry A. Murray have stated this point very forcibly with their observations that "culture acts as a set of blinders, or series of lenses, through which men view their environments." Further, they remark, "the skills that are acquired, the factual knowledge, the basic assumptions, the values, and the tastes, are largely determined by culture."[3]

By the time when psychology had developed the integrative concept of personality, deeply differentiated in different societies by diverse processes of socialization, and when anthropology had developed the integrative concept of culture, also differentiated in different societies and acting as the medium through which external conditions were transformed into determinants of personality, both were committed, implicitly, but inevitably, to a recognition of differentials in group character which could take the form of national character as readily as any form. The two were also on the brink of a major synthesis with each other—a synthesis whose importance has not been properly recognized outside the fields which were involved, although it may be regarded as one of the epic advances of modern social science. Psychology would find in the culture concept a key to the interaction between society and the individual. Anthropology would find in the personality concept a key to the process by which external circumstances are internalized in transmuted form as traits and qualities of the individual. Culture, the medium, and personality, the receptor, were indispensable, each to the other.

If we attempt to trace historically the actual execution of this synthesis, major attention must be given to the work of Leslie A. White, who published an article on "Personality and Culture" in 1925, and of Professor Edward Sapir, who, with the collaboration of John Dollard, conducted a seminar in culture and personality

3. *Personality in Nature, Society, and Culture* (New York: Alfred A. Knopf, 1949), pp. 45, 41.

at Yale University in 1932–33. W. I. Thomas, in work for the Social Science Research Council, also played an important part.

In 1933, writing on "Personality" in the *Encyclopaedia of the Social Sciences,* Sapir said: "The socialization of personality traits may be expected to lead cumulatively to the development of specific psychological biases in the cultures of the world. Thus, Eskimo culture, contrasted with most North American Indian cultures, is extraverted; Hindu culture on the whole corresponds to the world of the thinking introvert; the culture of the United States is definitely extraverted in character, with a greater emphasis on thinking and intuition than on feeling; and sensational evaluations are more clearly evident in the cultures of the Mediterranean area than in those of Northern Europe."

One could not ask for a more decisive or more dramatic indication of what had happened to the doctrine of national character than this. In the very same work in which the historian Max Hildebert Boehm wrote an obituary for the doctrine with his statement that during the nineteenth century "the idea of the character of an epoch came to displace that of national character," an anthropologist was reaffirming the validity of the doctrine and placing it for the first time on a tenable and scientific basis. It is for this reason that historians must make themselves aware of the findings of social psychology which Louis Wirth has recently described as "a general discipline basic to all of the social sciences."[4]

I suppose there can hardly be any question that this new culture-and-personality concept of the differentiation of groups is, for practical purposes, our old friend, national character, in more modern and considerably more decent dress. But, if there was any doubt to begin with, subsequent developments in this area of investigation have decisively established the recognition of nation-

4. Louis Wirth, "The Social Sciences," in Merle Curti (ed.), *American Scholarship in the Twentieth Century* (Cambridge, Mass.: Harvard University Press, 1953), p. 62.

al character. There were two developments, especially, which reinforced this point of view. One was the work of Ruth Benedict and Margaret Mead in attempting to perceive the dominating behavior patterns in any given culture and to interpret the people of the culture in terms of this dominant factor; this approach was brilliantly applied in Benedict's *Patterns of Culture* in 1934. The other was the work of Abram Kardiner, the psychoanalyst, who co-operated with Ralph Linton and others to analyze what they called the "basic personality structure." Where Benedict and Mead had resorted to the concept of *types,* against which they could measure specific individuals, Kardiner, whose work was in some respects an extension of the Gestalt idea, was concerned with finding the *norms* of personality, without the interposition either of behavioral data or of typological concepts. For, though the recognition of types might aid in classification, it was feared that it might also sway the subjective judgment of the investigator. Kardiner's approach is both so important and so precisely reasoned that it should be stated in his own words: "If," he says, "we can establish that similar projective systems operate in all individuals in a given society because the integrational systems are based on similar experiences from contact with institutions or practices followed by all members in the society, then we can not only account for similar dispositions in the individuals, but also for the specific needs of that society." Kardiner then continues to discuss the nature of various cultural institutions which may impinge upon the members of society and impose similar experiences upon them: "If childhood disciplines constitute one order of institutions then religion and folklore comprise another. We called the former primary and the latter secondary. Also, there was something created in the individual by his childhood experiences which formed the basis for the projective systems subsequently used to create folklore and religion. This group of nuclear constellations in the individual was designated the *basic personality structure*. This concept proved to be only a refinement of a concept long since used descriptively by Herodotus and Caesar and known as *national character*."[5]

Kardiner's eminent collaborator, Ralph Linton, was no less positive and explicit in accepting the validity of the concept of national character. Linton pointed out that "Rorschach series from different societies reveal different norms for such series as wholes," and he affirmed flatly that "it is a readily observable fact that the personality norms for different societies do differ."[6] Infact, he was markedly impatient with those who doubted, and he condemned "certain anthropologists" for failing to accept this frankly and for "trying to minimize the extent and importance of such differences. ... To believe that all human groups have the same psychological potentialities," he said, "without trying to account for their very obvious differences in overt behavior and even in value-attitude systems calls for a degree of faith in scientific authority of which few individuals are capable. Even general statements that the observed differences are due to cultural factors remain unconvincing as long as they are not accompanied by explanations of what these factors may be and how they operate."[7]

Virtually all the workers in this field have taken the same position. Otto Klineberg, in his *Tensions Affecting International Understanding* (1950), has discussed a wide variety of approaches to the subject of national differentiation and the techniques for appraising it. He has written a significantly titled article, "A Science of National Character,"[8] and Margaret Mead has written similarly on "The Study of National Character."[9] In 1949, Clyde Kluck-

5. *Op. cit.*, pp. 20, 23–24. The original formulation of the concept of "basic personality structure" appeared in Kardiner and Linton, *The Individual and His Society* (New York: Columbia University Press, 1939).

6. *The Cultural Background of Personality* (New York: D. Appleton–Century Co., 1945), p. 128.

7. *Ibid.*, pp. 138 ff.

8. *Journal of Social Psychology*, XIX (1944), 147–62.

9. In Daniel Lerner (ed.), *The Policy Sciences: Recent Developments in Scope and Method* (Stanford, Calif.: Stanford University Press, 1951).

hohn and Henry A. Murray asserted that "the statistical prediction can safely be made that a hundred Americans, for example, will display certain defined characteristics more frequently than will a hundred Englishmen comparably distributed as to age, sex, social class, and vocation." These authors ended the Introduction to their important book *Personality in Nature, Society, and Culture* by saying, "All research in this field is in the last analysis directly or indirectly oriented to one central type of question: What makes an Englishman an Englishman? An American an American? A Russian a Russian?"[10]

With this quotation, the argument may very well rest. After all its vicissitudes, national character is still with us. The fact is inescapable. But, we should hasten to observe, this is no longer the national character that we encountered in the previous chapter. That national character had never been defined or analyzed with precision, and it bristled with unresolved difficulties. There was no agreement as to its nature—whether changing or immutable, whether present in everyone or only in "typical" or representative individuals, whether absolute or variable. This uncertainty as to its nature was inescapable in view of the fact that its determinants were not understood. Because of this lack, many writers had accepted the fallacious explanations of racism, while others who avoided the errors of race were forced to fall back on environmental explanations which went astray because it had not been recognized either that the culture interposes between the individual and his physical environment or that the society itself has often erected a secondary environment more important than the original or primary one. Moreover, the concept of national character suffered from the facts (1) that it had failed to distinguish between character as a whole and the individual traits which were only parts or manifestations of character, (2) that it had failed to recognize the overlapping of various kinds of social groups (class groups, national groups, etc.) and the necessity for

10. *Op. cit.*, pp. xiv, 36, 39.

distinguishing between the traits of the national group and the traits that were attributable to other groupings, and (3) that it had been unable to define the geographical limits within which one national character could be said to exist.

The concept of national character which emerges from the culture-and-personality analysis is free of most of these difficulties, and consequently it has a great deal more value as a tool. To begin with, it clearly recognizes the determinant: the determinant is the culture, acting upon and shaping the personality, and though this may still leave an ultimate question (to which I shall return) as to what determines the culture, it clarifies a great deal that was previously in confusion. It means that national character is a changing and not a fixed quality, for the culture itself changes; it means also that national character varies from one individual to another, partly because no two personalities are enough alike to receive the impact of the culture in precisely the same way, but even more because the culture assigns diverse roles to various classes of individuals in the society, and it imposes different cultural experiences and makes different cultural demands upon each of these classes or status groups. Further, it means that no mystic link exists to unite race and character and that no direct relationship exists between environment and character, for, as Linton expressed it, "between the natural environment and the individual there is always interposed a human environment which is vastly more significant."

As for the other difficulties, much has been gained in clarifying them also. The systematic study of personality has not only eliminated the random consideration of separate traits but has also demonstrated that there are practical as well as theoretical advantages in dealing with the personality as a whole. One of the clearest demonstrations of these advantages appears in the study by T. W. Adorno and his collaborators on *The Authoritarian Personality*. The point of departure for Adorno's study was a concern with anti-Semitism, but he soon reached the conclusion that anti-Semitism is an aspect of a certain kind of personality structure and is not a separable quality in itself. The most crucial result of his vast and important investigation was the "demonstration of close correspondence in the type of approach and outlook [which] a subject is likely to have in a great variety of areas, ranging from the most intimate features of family and sex adjustment through relationships to other people in general, to religion and to social and political philosophy. Thus a basically hierarchical, authoritarian exploitive parent-child relationship is apt to carry over into a power-oriented, exploitively dependent attitude toward one's sex partner and one's God and may well culminate in a political philosophy and social outlook which has no room for anything but a desperate clinging to whatever appears to be strong and a disdainful rejection of whatever is relegated to the bottom."[11]

The implications of this statement are very extensive. for it indicates that many topics which have been regarded as subjects in themselves are in reality only aspects of some larger subject. Historians in general have been almost wholly oblivious to this consideration, and the literature of intellectual history abounds in monographs on particular intellectual attitudes such as anti-Semitism, fascism, or the like—monographs which treat the subject as if it could be understood by itself and at the rational or intellectual level. I will not labor this subject, but Adorno's statement casts doubt on the validity of scores of subjects of this kind and suggests that the whole basis for selecting specialized topics of research in social and intellectual history ought to be overhauled. For the immediate purposes of this discussion however, the ruling consideration is that the psychological study of character emphasizes the importance of bringing character as an entirety into its focus, in this way avoiding the erratic and fragmentary effect that results from pinning a full-scale characterological diagnosis upon some tag end of a personality trait.

11. T. W. Adorno *et. al.*, *The Authoritarian Personality* (New York: Harper & Bros., 1950), p. 971.

The concept of culture has also done much to organize an understanding of the relationship between the national grouping (with the character traits which pertain to it) and the other groupings (with the character traits which pertain to them) which overlap one another in most modern societies. History, as I have already indicated, has dealt with these relationships casually or not at all and has been prone to treat the attributes of any group as if they were the national attributes of the nation to which members of the group belonged. But the theory of basic personality structure carefully avoids these confusions and offers a fully effective theory for dealing with the problems involved. Linton, with characteristic force and precision, stated this theory in *The Cultural Background of Personality*. He began by stating the nature of the various groupings: "The individuals who compose . . . a society are classified and organized in several different ways simultaneously. Each of these systems has its own functions as regards relating the individual to culture, and he occupies a place within each of them. Thus every member of the society has a place in the age-sex system and also in the prestige series. He has a place in the system of specialized occupations. . . . He always belongs to some family unit and one or more association groups." Having postulated these groupings, Linton then went on to put the question "whether a given society should be thought of as having a single personality norm or as having a series of different personality norms each of which is associated with a particular status group within the society." The answer to this question, one might suppose, would not be the same for all nations and might depend upon the depth of class cleavages within the society. Linton was probably thinking of some such society as our own, therefore, when he observed that all the members of a society have "a long series of personality elements in common" and that they also have "additional configurations of responses [to be known as 'status personalities'] which are linked with certain socially delimited groups within the society."

But these status personalities, instead of standing separately from, or in contrast to, the national personality, he felt, were "superimposed upon its basic personality type and are thoroughly integrated with the latter."

Allowing as it does for the fact that "every society has its own basic personality type and its own series of status personalities differing in some respects from those of any other society,"[12] Linton's analysis certainly provides a rational schema, which was previously lacking, for the analysis of the traits in a given aggregation of people when these people have several group affiliations, to any of which the traits might be attributed.

A final difficulty in the concept of national character, as it was traditionally handled, centered in the problem of defining the unit within which national character may be said to exist. To cope with this problem, the reader will recall, Karl W. Deutsch, a political scientist, has proposed the formula that "membership in a people essentially consists in wide complementarity of social communication," which he considers a more reliable criterion than any set of specific ingredients such as common language, common memories, or the like. It is hard to see how anyone can disagree with this ably argued proposition, and one may even agree to the validity of conducting an incredibly large number of recordings of the frequency and intensity of communications in order to arrive at an objective measurement of complementarity. For many modern nations which are to some extent subdivisions of the one great culture known as "Western civilization," such measurements may be necessary. But it is worth noting that, where the culture is clearly defined, it takes care of the factor of "complementarity." Indeed, there are cultures which refuse to communicate at all with nonmembers, so that he who would communicate must first gain adoption into the tribe. The real significance of a common language is simply that it serves as a cultural device to facilitate complementarity

12. Quotations from pp. 75–76, 128–31.

within the culture and to interdict it outside the culture. Thus, it might be argued, complementarity is essentially a functional aspect of the common culture, and, in so far as it clarifies the problem, the culture concept is again basic to an improvement in the understanding of national character.

Such are the contributions of the personality-and-culture approach to the study of national character. Proponents of this approach have committed themselves unequivocally to the concept of national character. They have handled the concept with an analytical skill which, it must be admitted, historians never brought to bear. And it looks very much as though they have made their conclusions stick. It is true that special applications of their theory, such as Geoffrey Gorer's analysis of the Great Russians, have been subjected to devastating criticism, and there has been a certain amount of feuding between the psychoanalytic school and the school which relies upon "culture configuration."[13] Also, dispute is still current as to the relative importance of very early experience, such as toilet training, and later, more diffused experience, in the impingement of culture upon personality. But, even with full allowance for all these facts, it remains true that the study of national character is today in the custody of the behavioral scientists and that they have earned their primacy in this field.

Where does this leave the historians? Although I have spoken enthusiastically of the achievements of the behavioral scientists (and disparagingly of the work of the historians), I do not at all mean to concede that historians have nothing to contribute or that they must sit at the feet of workers in other disciplines. On the contrary, I believe that there should be a reciprocal depend-

13. Mead speaks of three distinctive approaches: one which emphasizes the configuration of the culture as a whole, another which focuses upon the relation between the basic learning of the child and other aspects of his culture, and a third which relies upon the systematic study of patterns of interpersonal relationships between parent and child, peer and peer, etc. (*op. cit.*, p. 81).

ence between historians and other investigators, the need for which has not been adequately recognized on either side, and that this failure of each to utilize what the other might contribute has hampered the rounded development of the subject. I will return to this theme and will seek to prove this proposition in the final section of this chapter. But, before entering this phase of the subject, it may be well to turn from the long theoretical discussion which has occupied this chapter so far and to examine some of the concrete analyses of the American character which have been made by leading behavioral scientists. Let us therefore consider, as well as we can in such brief compass, three such interpretations, all relying on the concepts of culture and personality, but written from the three specific standpoints of cultural anthropology, social psychology, and psychoanalysis.

Although it did not come first chronologically, we may turn first to the interpretation developed by Margaret Mead in a number of writings and set forth in particularly explicit terms in *And Keep Your Powder Dry* (New York: William Morrow & Co., 1942). Miss Mead is one of the best-known exponents of the approach of cultural anthropology, and yet it would be too much to say that she represents the cultural anthropologists, for she is, as Clyde Kluckhohn has remarked, "a controversial figure, both within the anthropological profession and in intellectual circles generally." Yet, he has also observed, "there are grounds for suspecting that the emotional heat of many critiques of Margaret Mead's and Geoffrey Gorer's books was generated less by righteous indignation at careless scholarship and fuzzy logic than by fury against the raising of certain personal and cultural issues comfortably buried in the unconscious."[14] It may be that what he calls anthropology's "return from the natives" has been too abrupt, and the cultural approach does not have to stand or fall upon the success of Mead's application of it;

14. Clyde Kluckhohn, "Anthropology Comes of Age," *American Scholar*, XIX (1950), 241 ff.

but there are many reasons for taking her interpretation very seriously.

The first important aspect of Mead's interpretation, as it impinges upon my discussion here, is her reaffirmation of a concept of national character, as a reality and not an illusion. "In every culture," she says, "in Samoa, in Germany, in Iceland, in Bali, and in the United States of America, we will find consistencies and regularities in the way in which new-born babies grow up and assume the attitudes and behavior patterns of their elders—and this we may call 'character formation.' We will find that Samoans may be said to have a Samoan character structure and Americans an American character structure. Banishing the bogies of racism and its related inconsistencies does not mean that we must end up by saying that all peoples are alike just because we believe that within a normal distribution of individual differences and potentialities more or less common to each group, they *could* have been alike under other circumstances."

As she turns to the analysis of the American character structure, her strongest emphasis falls upon the way in which American life is geared to success rather than to status. That is, the American measures his own worth by the distance which he has progressed from his point of departure rather than by the position which he occupies; he esteems high current income more than the possession of long-accumulated wealth. He is keenly aware of class distinctions and class levels, which are powerful realities in America, though they lack the tangibility of such distinctions in the Old World, but he conceives of the class hierarchy as a ladder whose rungs are to be ascended rather than as a set of pigeonholes whose compartments are identified with permanent status. Projecting this success drive to his children, he expects them to have a different future and an achievement greater than his own. Mobility and change are natural by-products of his quest for success, and departure from the patterns of the past is a matter of course.

From this abandonment of traditional ways and from the mobility of individuals, there results a second feature, and this is the American's excessive concern with conformity. For instance, when a man and wife of diverse national backgrounds marry and have children, the chances are that they have no personal standards of child-rearing to which they can cling. Both, in becoming Americans, have rejected the standards of the culture from which they came, and, because of the diversity of their backgrounds, they are unlikely in any case to have standards in common. Hence the only standard to which they can resort is the practice of their neighbors, whose opinion often gains such a tyrannical ascendancy over them that the child is judged in terms of his success in meeting the standard instead of the standard's being judged in terms of its success in developing the child. In a traditional culture, the parents would unquestioningly apply traditional standards, blissfully unaware of possible alternatives and with fatalistic acceptance of whatever might result in the child. But in the American culture they anxiously look to the child to excel the neighbor's children, thus to vindicate their training, and also to prove that he is going to be a success.

One of the ideas which Mead has most effectively impressed upon the public is a realization of the way in which infant training fixes many traits of character which endure throughout life. This is, of course, an important concept in the study of the manner in which the culture operates upon the personality. When an infant is reared under the conditions I have just described, he senses very early that his progress is watched with a certain anxiety and that the manifestations of love from his parents correspond in some measure to what he achieves. Hence he is stimulated to excel and thus is prepared very early for participation in a highly competitive society, in which failure, even though cushioned by a good standard of living, seems more terrible than poverty itself would seem in a status society.

Mead does not attempt a systematic analysis of the determinants or causes of the character which she describes. But she does make very fruitful suggestions, and one of these is her statement that "we are all third generation," not, of course, in the literal sense but in the sense that all of us have the attitude of the third-generation American. The first-generation immigrant clings to his traditional ways, while ceasing to honor them; the second-generation American performs the act of rejection, finding it a bitter struggle to do so; the third-generation individual finds that his act of rejection is almost expected of him, and without friction he is launched by his parents into the competition for success, in which he is required to go beyond them in perfecting his conformity to American ways and in winning the approbation of his American neighbors.[15]

Geoffrey Gorer expresses this same general idea in an even more pointed way, but without Mead's care to avoid pitfalls. For instance, he says, "It is this break of continuity between the immigrants of the first generation and their children of the second generation which is to my mind of major importance in the development of the modern American character."[16]

Bearing in mind this anthropological interpretation and its "third-generation" hypothesis, let us now turn to a second treatment of the American character, this time by a social psychologist. This is David Riesman's interpretation, as set forth in *The Lonely Crowd: A Study of the Changing American Character* (New Haven: Yale University Press, 1950). *The Lonely Crowd* is not a study of national character in the conventional sense, partly because it does not emphasize the distinctiveness of Americans as compared with Europeans but accepts the American as "a subtype of a generalized Western European industrial

15. Mead, *And Keep Your Powder Dry*, esp. pp. 20–21, 31, 40–41, 50–53, 86–91.
16. *The American People: A Study in National Character* (New York: W. W. Norton & Co., 1948), p. 26.

type." Nor does it focus upon the specific qualities or traits of character which are formed in the American; instead, its attention is directed to "the modes of conformity in the several successive stages of our western society." It is a book, as Riesman says, "about the nature of the processes that produce . . . differences in character." In short, it deals not with a specific catalogue of *traits* but with the diverse ways in which individuals at various stages of society have formed different *systems of values*.

Throughout life the individual is confronted by an endless series of alternatives or choices in matters both trivial and important. These choices range from the selection of dishes on a menu to the decision on a proposal of marriage. No person can possibly deal with all these decisions on their merits or even on an *ad hoc* basis; he must constantly have at hand a set of ready-made values which can be applied in disposing of most of the choices automatically. How does man acquire this set of values today, and has he always acquired them in the same way? This is the principal question which *The Lonely Crowd* attempts to answer.

As Riesman sees it, this process of value-formation has passed through three major stages. In the Middle Ages, when society was largely static, continuity strong, and the social pattern relatively simple, specific responses could be learned for most of the situations that were likely to arise in life. These responses had been transmitted in a context of tradition until they became standard and were memorized, so to speak, by the individual, who could therefore properly be described as a "tradition-directed man." But later, in the early industrial phase, when society became more dynamic, more complex, and more subject to innovations, it was no longer possible to learn a specific response for every situation. The nearest possible equivalent was to learn a set of fixed principles that would be applicable for any situation and to instil these principles into the individual during his early training. Such principles were implanted in the "conscience," or "superego," by parents or other elders, and, once instilled, they served as a stabilizer or gyroscope governing the individual's conduct. Hence he was "inner-directed." This inner-directed man was content to go his own way, to pursue his own hobbies, to commune with himself, and, if need be, to stand out against the entire community. The American of the nineteenth century was usually inner-directed.

By the mid-twentieth century, however, social mutation had become both rapid and violent, and values were increasingly relative rather than absolute. Moreover, economic changes placed an ever growing proportion of people in employment where their success depended not upon winning mastery of the physical environment (which had been the great objective of the nineteenth century) but upon gaining the favor of other individuals, upon winning friends and influencing people. In such a situation, inflexible principles and disdain for the shifts of public opinion were liabilities rather than assets, and a new adjustment began to be made. In this adjustment, the individual no longer followed the dictates of conscience but instead became highly responsive to the fluctuations and cross-currents of day-to-day opinion, as well as to the momentary standards of any group with which he was momentarily associated. He was now equipped with a radar screen instead of a gyroscope, and he could properly be described as "other-directed." As such, he had no "internalized" values of his own but altered his behavior, his opinions, his activities, his manners, and his entire way of life to gain the approval of those around him. Like Willy Loman, in *Death of a Salesman*, he felt it tremendously important to be "well liked." He could no longer feel, as did the inner-directed man, satisfaction in adhering to standards of his own even in the face of community opposition; instead, he sought anxiously for the approbation of the group. In this country, with its mobility, its continuing rapid transformation, and its tradition of the prompt acceptance of what is up to date, the American has became pre-eminently an other-directed man.

More than most analysts of contemporary American society, Riesman gives recognition to the play of historical forces. Obviously, the changes in the tempo and the complexity of life, and the shift from success through the conquest of nature to success through winning the good will of others, are themselves of a historical nature. Moreover, Riesman is particularly sensitive to the multiplicity of factors present in any given social situation. Yet, when he comes to the point of offering a causal analysis for the various phases of direction, he appears to commit himself very heavily to one single factor, namely, the rate of population growth. In his own words, "I . . . have chosen to emphasize some possible relationships between the population growth of a society and the historical sequence of character types." Developing this thesis, he defines three phases of population growth. The first, characteristic of primitive societies, is marked by a high birth rate, and a high death rate balancing the birth rate, and is designated as a society of "high growth potential." The second phase occurs when discoveries in hygiene or other improvements in living cause a drop in the death rate and a consequent rapid increase in population; this phase is said to be one of "transitional growth." Finally, societies where the birth rate has declined to restore a balance with the death rate have arrived at a third phase—one of "incipient population decline." Having enumerated these phases, he then asserts their determinative function in producing tradition-directed, inner-directed, and other-directed men. As he states the relationship, "the society of high growth potential develops in its typical members a social character whose conformity is insured by their tendency to follow tradition: these I shall term *tradition-directed* people." Having said so much for the tradition-directed, he twice repeats the causal statement that "the society of transitional population growth" or of "incipient population decline" "develops in its typical members a social character" that is either inner-directed or other-directed. Let me add that Riesman takes pains to recognize that "change in the population age distribution,

even with all it implies . . . cannot determine character all by itself," but clearly he regards it as highly important.[17]

Thus we have two interpretations which approach national
character from the standpoint of anthropology and of social
psychology. To these let us add a third and final one, from the
standpoint of psychoanalysis.

This third interpretation was set forth by Dr. Karen Horney
in *The Neurotic Personality of Our Time* (1937). At first glance,
it might appear that Horney was discussing psychopathology
rather than national character, and I do not believe she used the
word "American" anywhere in her book. But her whole conten-
tion was that psychoanalysis has overemphasized "the biological
origin of mental characteristics" and has erred in attributing
"social phenomena primarily to psychic factors and these primarily to biological factors." For, as she saw it, "when we realize
the great import of cultural conditions on neuroses, the biological
and physiological conditions which are considered by Freud to
be their root recede into the background."

Horney did not deny, of course, that individual experiences
are critical in generating neuroses, but she contended that "specific cultural conditions under which we live" are also critical.
Indeed, it is the cultural conditions which "in the last analysis
determine their particular form" of the neurosis. For example, she
said, "It is an individual fate . . . to have a domineering or a 'self-
sacrificing' mother, but it is only under definite cultural conditions that we find domineering or self-sacrificing mothers." The
wide applicability of the same cultural conditions makes for a
similarity in the neuroses which appear in the culture, and, though
neuroses may be very dissimilar in their symptoms or their
mechanisms, "the crucial conflicts around which a neurosis grows
are practically always the same."

Hence, in speaking of a neurotic personality of our time, she
meant not only that "there are neurotic persons having essential
peculiarities in common, but also that these basic similarities are

17. *Op. cit.*, esp. pp. 3–31.

essentially produced by the difficulties existing in our time and culture." Furthermore, the problems of the neurotic person "differ only in quantity from the problems bothering the normal person in our culture."

Is not this equivalent to saying that society in this country presents characteristic problems which produce characteristic human adjustments or maladjustments? And does not the recurrence in America of these patterned adjustments and maladjustments as group rather than purely individual phenomena constitute what we mean by "national character"?

Horney's striking observations inevitably raise the question, "What are the conditions in the culture which produce such problems and conflicts for the individual, and what is their impact upon the normal as well as upon the neurotic person?" The answers could perhaps best be given by the sociologist, and Horney modestly deferred to him for a definitive answer; but she indicated in a final chapter, as clear as it is brief, "the main trends" which, she believed, "have a bearing on the problem of neurosis and culture." First she discussed one basic source of stress and then a number of cultural dilemmas or sources of inner conflict for the individual.

The fundamental stress is the strong emphasis upon the principle of individual competition in modern society—a principle which is economically based but which extends to such highly personal values as popularity and attractiveness and which impinges on the individual in infancy, at school, and as an adult—in relation to parents, with spouse, and with offspring: "Competitive stimuli are active from the cradle to the grave."

Briefly, what is the effect of this condition? Competition, said Horney, means rivalry, and rivalry carries with it hostile tension between rivals. Hostile tension produces fear of others, and it also produces fear of failure. These fears weaken the self-esteem of the individual, and weakened self-esteem leads to an excessive craving for love.

The cultural dilemmas spoken of in her discussion are important, because "in every neurosis" there are not only stresses and problems but also "contradictory tendencies which the neurotic is unable to reconcile." Are these contradictions internal, personal, and imaginary, or are they external, cultural, and real? Very often, she affirmed, society imposes the dilemma, and it is a real one. Three such dilemmas are especially prevalent in our society today: one is the obligation imposed upon the individual, on the one hand, to manifest enough aggressiveness to assure his own success in competition and, on the other, to manifest Christian consideration, humility, and brotherly love for other people; a second is the way in which rivalry in consumption stimulates our need and desire for goods to a point so high that the majority experience frustration in attaining it; a third is the discrepancy between the theoretical freedom of the individual and the actual limitations which restrict him. "These contradictions, embedded in our culture, are precisely the conflicts which the neurotic struggles to reconcile: his tendencies toward aggressiveness and his tendencies toward yielding; his excessive demands and his fear of never getting anything; his striving toward self-aggrandizement and his feeling of personal helplessness. The difference from the normal is merely quantitative."[18]

Here, then, we have an anthropologist, a social psychologist, and a psychoanalyst, all generalizing very broadly about the distinctive personality traits which prevail in our culture—that

18. Horney, *op. cit.*, esp. pp. vii, viii, 14–33, 281–89. Cf. the following statement from Franz Alexander, *Our Age of Unreason* (Philadelphia: J. B. Lippincott, 1942): "A specialist of emotional disturbances practicing at the present day in this country who attempts to help his patient by the method of psychoanalysis is inevitably impressed by the frequency of one kind of conflict. The patients are driven by a relentless competitiveness in any given field and are at the same time afraid and wearied by this strenuous life of race and struggle, are tortured by insecurity and secretly want in their hearts, more than any thing else, rest and security. . . . Those of us who have had the opportunity to study patients in other cultural environments are particularly impressed by the frequency and intensity of this conflict between ambition and dependence in present-day America" (p. 307).

is, as an earlier generation would have said, about our national character. We must bear in mind, of course, that their report is not a unanimous one. Other anthropologists, social psychologists, and psychoanalysts have voiced dissenting opinions and have made criticisms which it would be worth while to examine if there were space to do so. But, without ignoring such criticisms, I believe it is entirely just to say that these new investigators have reaffirmed the concept of national character and have successfully met most of the difficulties which I discussed previously. First of all, they have been at great pains to demonstrate, at the purely expository level, that uniformities of attitude and behavior actually exist and thus that national character is verifiable as a factual reality. Second, by their attention to the culture, they have explored the medium within which national character develops and have provided a basis for regarding it, as it should be regarded, as a relative rather than as an absolute quality, altering gradually in response to changing conditions and manifesting itself as a tendency in the majority of members of the national group rather than as a universal attribute present in all of them. Further, the emphasis upon culture has freed the concept of national character from the curse of racism, for culture finds the continuum in the complex of social custom and not in the genes. Still further, these writers are all subtle and perceptive interpreters of the complexities of social culture and individual personality, and thus they avoid the errors of crude environmentalism, which so often failed to understand the workings of the human receptors upon which environmental forces operated. Also, they are acutely conscious of the secondary environment, and, indeed, one of Riesman's chief contributions is in tracing the effects of the change from an environment that motivated the individual as producer to one that motivates him as consumer.

In a strict sense, of course, these writers are concerned with cultural character (just as earlier writers were concerned, literally, with ethnic character), and their interpretations are not "national," except in so far as the culture unit is related to and equated with the national unit. No doubt the degree to which the national unit in a political sense corresponds to a culture unit will vary widely from country to country, and one may doubt whether the people of some nations, such as the countries of Central America or the Moslem kingdoms of the Near East, constitute real culture units or have national characters which seem very distinctive when compared with adjoining peoples. Also, one may doubt whether, given the technology of the present world, any nation has as distinctive a culture as nations used to have. But, historically, the nation is often the political manifestation of the impulse toward unity in a culture group, and the cultural character is therefore likely also to be the national character. This identity of the two is explicit in Mead's and Riesman's interpretations, and to me it seems clearly implicit in that of Horney.

These three interpretations not only present a triad of diverse and rewarding insights; they also illuminate one subject—that of the American character—from the points of view of three different though related fields of study and with the method of three different disciplines. Thus they afford a tempting opportunity for triangulation: even more important than what they indicate individually is what they reveal in common. Do they merely offer a choice between three irreconcilable views, or is there a basic consistency in them? Does each have its own separate terminus, or do all lead the reader, by separate paths, to the same destination?

Since each one is formulated in its own anthropological, psychological, or psychoanalytical terms, there is naturally an appearance of diversity, so that one may not at first be aware to how great an extent they are saying the same thing. Mead's concern with our mobility and success drive; Riesman's concern with our dependence upon the esteem and the opinions of our peers; and Horney's concern with the dilemmas implicit in our culture are superficially not altogether homogeneous. But in essence they do, to a great extent, converge.

The common ground of the three may be found primarily, I suggest, in their emphasis upon the effects of the competitive spirit. The underlying importance of this competitive factor is readily evident in the explicit statements of each of these writers, but, to clinch the matter, let us glance at the main points in their analyses. In Mead's interpretation, we find stress upon success, upon mobility, upon American conformity, upon our tendency to push children into precocity. The success cult simply affirms that the attainment of the competitive goal is more important than the attainment of personal satisfaction; mobility simply says that the competitive race shall have no finishing post; conformity requires the individual to show his belief in the competitive system not only by embracing its goals but also by embracing all the physical impedimenta and behavior codes which are associated with these goals; the demands upon children to demonstrate their superiority mark the extension of the competitive race so that it is no longer a mere lifetime affair but becomes a relay contest extending over two or more generations.

In Riesman's discussion of the shift from the inner-directed to the other-directed personality, the basic emphasis is again upon competition, and the real change is that the means to the attainment of competitive success have changed. In an earlier time, when most men worked for themselves and were concerned with subduing the environment, the traits of the inner-directed man—stamina, determination, unremitting industry—were at a premium in competition. But in a society where the majority now work for others, where service bulks large in the economy, and where wealth is gained more readily by organizing and manipulating other men than by further raids upon nature, the traits of popularity, persuasiveness, attractiveness—"personality," as it is called—have become essential competitive equipment, and the "other-directed" man has forged to the front.

The factor of competition also runs through Horney's discussion, as I have already observed, and underlies her analysis. For instance, in each of her three dilemmas it is competition which causes inner conflicts by overtraining people for the competitive trial: it fits them for rivalry by stimulating an aggressiveness which the Christian tradition requires them to curb; it tempts them by promising greater material awards than the economy can confer; it stimulates them by assuring them of a freedom which is never to be realized.

Drawing these three interpretations together, then, we have three treatments which agree, or may be construed as agreeing, that the American character is in a large measure a group of responses to an unusually competitive situation. Competition may be factored out time and again as a common denominator, and thus one arrives at an important and encouraging conclusion: in the realm of observation and description, these three studies, though of diverse origin and written in the idiom of diverse disciplines, reinforce and corroborate one another in their findings as to the essential elements of the American character.

If we turn from description to causal analysis, however, the results are far less easy to relate, for the writers under review are not primarily concerned with determinative forces. Their vital purpose is to arrive at an objective measure of the traits that exist, rather than to explain the origin of such traits. Consequently, the explanations which they offer are rather secondary and are not worked out in analytical detail. Since these explanations are offered incidentally to the exposition, it would be unfair to treat them as essential parts of the studies under consideration; but, at the same time, it is clearly necessary for our purposes to observe that, unlike the descriptions, they are somewhat inconsistent with one another and, moreover, that they are open to certain criticisms.

Horney did not attempt to formulate an explanation, which she believed must be derived from sociology, but like a good medical practitioner she was content to refer the case to a sociological specialist for consultation.

Riesman explains character in terms of population phase and offers the proposition that a "society of incipient population decline develops in its typical members a social character" that is other-directed. If we confine our view to the United States alone, this statement would seem applicable, for certainly this country is in the population phase of incipient decline and certainly the other-directed person is typical in America if he is typical anywhere. But there is a real question whether there are not other countries in which the phase of incipient decline is even more clearly established, without any corresponding prevalence of other-directed persons. England is in this phase; so is France, and France has been in it for many decades longer than we. But does the typical Englishman have a character that is other-directed? Does the typical Frenchman? I do not know how Riesman would answer this question, but most people, I believe, would say "No."

Mead explains character in terms of the immigrant break with tradition. Unlike the first and second generations, which have either clung to their hereditary culture or have experienced guilt in abandoning it, the third generation, having learned to break with the past, continues to embrace what is new and even honors it for its "up-to-dateness," just as traditionalists honor the old for its antiquity. Hence the emphasis upon progress, mobility, and change and hence the readiness of the American to conform to the standards of his neighbors, even though they are at variance with the standards of his own upbringing. Again, if we confine our view to the United States, this formula seems to fit exactly; certainly it describes the process of "Americanization" through which millions of immigrant families have passed. But in other parts of the New World, immigrant groups have conspicuously failed to conform to this process. The habitans of Quebec, for instance, and the Hispanic population in Costa Rica, like the people of the United States, spring from forebears who were wrenched loose and uprooted from the Old World; but they clearly do not have the traits which the people of the United

States are said to derive from this ancestral experience. They remain, in a sense, creoles, and creoles all over the world, like Bourbons, are prone to be more royalist than the king. To this point, I suppose the rebuttal might be offered that, though the creole and the immigrant in the melting pot have both been transported, they are dissimilar in that the creole has never been impelled to make the first break with his native tradition, while the immigrant has. The distinction, certainly, is valid; but does it not require us to focus our attention less upon the immigrant and more upon the conditions in the American culture which cause immigrants—and other people—to abandon their tradition?

It deserves repeating that these three notable studies which I am attempting to discuss do not stand or fall on anything they may say as to the determining forces that have produced the American character which they describe. For they do not undertake, primarily, to solve problems of causation. Where earlier writers tried first of all to prove the validity of a causal force and thence to infer that such a force must have resulted in a national character, these behavioral scientists are perhaps more concerned with establishing the existence of such a character and ascertaining its nature than with explaining it in any ultimate sense. This is, in all probability, an excellent corrective for the former situation, in which historians, geographers, climatologists, and so on, were so busy constructing hypotheses to explain national character that they did not trouble to verify the existence of what they were explaining.

But, though desirable as an offset to previous tendencies, this inclination to take the culture as a given factor and to explain character in terms of the culture without very much systematic consideration of the forces which determined the culture—this tendency is a limiting factor which, in the last analysis, would interfere with the deepest and fullest understanding of society. The determinants of the culture must themselves be introduced fully and carefully into the analysis, and it is at this point, if anywhere, that history should re-enter the picture.

In the formulation of theory no one has for a moment denied that history has a function, and, if the historian is not included on the behavioral team, it is perhaps partly because he was not interested or because he saw no solution to the difficult problem of adapting his discipline to this kind of study. The importance of the historical factor has consistently been asserted by various behavioral scientists. Linton spoke of culture as "the precipitate of history," and in a series of definitions of culture he consistently included the historical element. His close associate, Abram Kardiner, ended the volume on *The Psychological Frontiers of Society* with a chapter on "Basic Personality and History," and he promised a future volume which would deal principally with historical aspects. In their recent treatise on *Character and Social Structure* (1953), Hans Gerth and C. Wright Mills have also given full emphasis to history. In fact, Robert K. Merton, in a Foreword to the book, introduces it with the observation that, while the psychological nature of social interaction has been closely studied, we have lacked any comparably intensive studies of "the psychological nature of the major social institutions that constitute the historically significant forms of such interaction," e.g., religion, business, etc. It is the chief objective of *Character and Social Structure*, he observes, "to present a systematic statement of just this approach, one in which political, economic, military, religious, and kinship institutions, and their historical transformations are connected with the character and personality, with the private as well as the public lives, of those living in the society. This book might therefore be described as an historically oriented psychology of social institutions."[19]

An element of major importance in this work of Gerth and Mills is that they refuse to accept any assumption as to which areas of interaction between persons are critical in the formation of personality, and hence they bring into their orbit certain areas such as the political and the military, which have seldom received attention at the hands of the behavioral scientists but which have

19. (New York: Harcourt, Brace & Co., 1953), p. vii.

long been accepted as fields for historical investigation. They assert that they "cannot rest content with the assumption that the kinship order, with its tensions of early love and authority, is necessarily the basic and lasting factor in the formation of personality; and that other orders of society are projective systems from this. . . . The father may not be the *primary* authority, but rather the replica of the power relations of society." Hence all these power relations must be set forth and analyzed in a systematic way. Analysis of this kind obviously begins to converge with the analysis which historians are quite accustomed to conducting in the study of power, its shifting locus and its distribution.

To repeat, I believe that behavioral scientists and historians have always been willing to undertake concerted effort and have been aware of the theoretical links between their disciplines. For example, in Caroline Ware's *The Cultural Approach to History* (New York: Columbia University Press, 1940), Goodwin Watson argued that history and psychology both deal with the same subject matter, namely, individual and social motivation and conduct, and that the only real difference between them lies in the size of the sample with which each one works. In the same symposium Franz Alexander emphasized the reciprocal dependence of history and psychology. "No individual," he said, "can be understood without knowing the social scene in which he lives and which has molded his personality, but no historical event can be understood without knowing the fundamental principles of human motivation, which are the dynamic driving force behind the ever-shifting scenes of history."[20]

Until the behavioral scientist finds a way to reinforce his structures with historical girders and until the historian learns to mix his paints with psychological oils, however, such statements seem likely to remain at the level of what has been called "verbal hat-

20. Watson, "Clio and Psyche: Some Interrelations of Psychology and History," pp. 34–37; Alexander, "Psychology and the Interpretation of Historical Events," pp. 48–57.

tipping." For the factor that has kept the behavioral scientist and the historian apart has not been the generic dissimilarity of their subject matter; it has been the difference in the area in which they operate. The behavioral scientist has found that three of the most critical theaters for his observation are the nursery, the bathroom, and the bedroom. The historian has not necessarily doubted the significance of the transactions that took place in these milieus, but he has never been able to align his historical sights on these targets. Even though he be a social or intellectual historian, he is still rather heavily concerned with public rather than private aspects of thought and conduct. From the nature of the materials with which he works this is likely to remain his situation, but this fact should not segregate the usefulness of his work unless we suppose that the public and general aspects of human experience are unrelated to the private and individual aspects.

To a behavioral scientist who, seeking the determinants of personality, scanned no horizon more remote than the infant's toilet chair, history, of course, could offer nothing relevant. But there were perhaps never so many behavioral scientists with this perspective as one may have supposed, and they definitely are growing fewer. Again, it is worth calling attention to the significance of the approach of Gerth and Mills. They devote substantial space to social orders, such as the religious order, the economic order, the political order, the military order, and the educational order, for which the data is essentially historical, and they argue cogently for a recognition of the interplay between these public orders and the private spheres upon which the study of personality has focused. To borrow one example, modern war, requiring mass armies, impinges upon the economic order by removing men from employment or unemployment, and it has repercussions in the sphere of private life by creating scarcity of potential husbands and by leaving families without fathers, girls without boys, and mothers without sons. "The structural and historical features of modern society," they say, "must be connected with the most intimate features of man's self."[21] Their statement, reposing quietly in the middle of a paragraph, does not resemble a manifesto on the relation of history to the behavioral sciences, but it is possible that it may turn out to be one.

Many illustrations might be cited to prove that public institutions such as the political regime, the military system, or the religious order may profoundly influence the values of a people. These institutions are the stuff of history, and a historian might have been expected to furnish the demonstration. Yet, paradoxically, it has taken an anthropologist to provide what is possibly the clearest and most convincing proof of this point: Douglas G. Haring, in a recent article, "Japanese National Character: Cultural Anthropology, Psychoanalysis, and History,"[22] compares the rigidity, formalism, and compulsiveness of the main body of Japanese, who have lived under a harsh dictatorship for three hundred years, with the spontaneity and permissiveness of the Japanese on the island of Amami Oshima, who escaped the authoritarian rule that prevailed elsewhere. He concludes that "in the formation of national character, police coercion shapes and outweighs infant training. Police tyranny is a fearful thing; it eliminates everyone who fails to adopt habits of conformity, suspicion, and tense watchfulness." Police tyranny is, of course, as distinctively a matter for the historian as infant training is a matter for the anthropologist. But it would be an error to establish a division between the two, for past history ultimately controlled our present infant training as surely as our present infant training may control future history.

If history, in fact, bears any relationship to the behavioral sciences in the study of man, its function must be primarily, as I have suggested, to identify and explain the determinants of the culture, and especially of cultural change. We have already noted that, while three brilliant expositors of the American culture have written accounts that harmonized strikingly in their analysis of

21. Gerth and Mills, *op. cit.*, p. xix.
22. *Yale Review*, XLII (1953), 375–92.

the culture itself, they diverged widely in their analysis of determinants—one invoking the uprooting of the immigrant as a factor, another stressing the factor of population growth. In a field of study where the recognition of multiplicity is essential, it would be foolish to deny the applicability of these factors, though, as we have seen, they present certain problems. And it would be absurd to suggest that some other single hidden factor is *the* factor—a kind of Public Enemy Number One for which the academic dragnet is out. Semantics is not yet enough of a science for us to know how many factors might legitimately be suggested. But, in the quest for a common denominator which might fit the analyses of Mead, Riesman, and Horney, it may be worth while to consider as a determinant the factor of economic abundance— not the abundance of locked-up natural resources to which man lacks the technological key but the abundance of usable goods produced from these resources—which the people of the United States have possessed in far greater degree than any other national population. The conspicuous importance of this factor has been recognized by countless writers, but its effects and its influence have received hardly any sustained and systematic consideration, and we may gain a further insight by examining its applicability here.

Later I should like to consider a little more fully the nature, the extent, and the historical character of this abundance; but for immediate purposes it suffices to note that, by the general consent of all observers, this state of relative abundance, of material plenty, has been a basic condition of American life and that it has had a pervasive, if undefined, influence upon the American people. Neither Mead, Riesman, nor Horney takes account of it specifically as a determinant that will help to explain the character traits which any one of them is describing, yet I think it can be shown that abundance plays an important part in each of the three descriptions and serves further to integrate the three as complementary analyses of the same basic structure.

How does abundance apply to the character portrayed by

Mead? One of her central ideas, as we have observed, is that in America, where we have a supremely strong compulsion to achieve success, this success is measured not by what one possesses in wealth or position but by what one has gained; it is not attainment of a fixed goal but advancement to a higher level. Certainly one reason for this attitude is that advancement has been gained by enough people to create a popular impression that it is a normal process and that those who fail to share in it are at fault personally. But the reason that people have been able to meet the expectation—and thereby to strengthen it in the minds of others—is that the constant opening of new areas, development of new resources, and discovery of new technological devices have provided a constant succession of new fields in which the individual could advance fairly readily and have produced a steady increase in the standard of living. This rise is so clearly evident that Chester W. Wright has been able to trace it in detail and make it the central focus of the presentation in his *Economic History of the United States* (New York: McGraw-Hill Book Co., Inc., 1941). Like a tide, it has carried most of the swimmers quickly forward to new marks.

As abundance raised the standard of living, however, it did far more than multiply the existing kinds of goods. It caused us to use new goods, new sources of energy, new services, and, by doing so, it transformed our way of life more than once every generation. Not to labor the point, let me simply observe that two centuries ago our structural materials were wood, brick, and stone and our sources of energy were wind in the sail, water in the wheel, and the animate muscle of men and beasts. Since then, we have exploited the revolutionary possibilities of iron and steel and have advanced into an era of synthetic materials; in terms of power, the age of steam has passed its zenith, yielding to the dynamo and the internal-combustion engine, which, in turn, seem to be yielding ground to the jet engine and the atomic pile. Of course, all the world has participated more or less in these changes, but the immense potential ready at hand in the United States has caused change to occur faster and to proceed further here than in other countries, so that every generation may be said to have erected a new world—a new secondary environment —undreamed of by the generation preceding. It is this constant change, paced by our economic richness, which, as I believe, has caused each generation to reject its predecessor and to expect its successor to reject it. This coincides with another of Miss Mead's points: the American rejection of the past as a projection of the immigrant's abandonment of the Old World. I would not minimize this important factor, but I would argue that, whereas our forebears have abandoned only one Europe, they have abandoned several outmoded Americas—frontier America, rural America, the isolated America of the river steamboat and the iron horse —and each abandonment has made us more ready to expect another. If we speak of father-rejection, has not the American with Colonial forebears rejected his American Puritan father even more decisively than the Irish-American has rejected his overseas father on the "Ould Sod"? Is not this the vital distinction between the immigrant to North America and the immigrant to Costa Rica, whose separation from the Old World has not perceptibly shaken his reliance upon traditional ways? Here, again, has not rapid social change, paced by economic abundance, rather than immigrant adjustment per se, been at the heart of the matter?

Riesman's concept of the other-directed man presents a rather different approach to the American character, but it, too, can be linked by a very definite sequence to the element of abundance. Indeed, Riesman, who is expert in historical matters, makes the connection himself, though in my opinion he does not exploit it fully. He observes that in most countries the margin of economic surplus is so narrow that every effort to increase the nation's assets of productive capacity and capital goods must involve a severe reduction in the current standard of living. Accordingly, one cannot expect the kind of increase in the supply of food and other commodities that will stimulate migration from country to city or replacement of the large, extended family by the small family. Hence the people of a country like France, limited by such conditions, continue to follow the ways of an inner-directed society, even though they have entered the phase of incipient population decline. But in America, Canada, and Australia, where European techniques can be applied to native resources, the transition becomes rapid and relatively easy.

Prior to the attainment of abundance, Riesman remarks, people are concerned primarily with increasing production. In their own temperament this requires hard enduringness and enterprise; in their external concerns it requires concentration upon dominating the physical environment; in their personal economy it requires thrift, prudence, abstinence. But once abundance is secured, the scarcity psychology which was once so valuable no longer operates to the advantage of society, and the ideal individual develops the qualities of the good consumer rather than those of the good producer. He needs now to cultivate interests that are appropriate to an enlarged leisure, and, since he is likely to be an employee rather than an entrepreneur or to be engaged in one of the service trades rather than in production, the cordiality of his relations with other people becomes more important than his mastery of the environment. In his personal economy, society expects him to consume his quota of goods—of automobiles, of whiskey, of television sets—by maintaining a certain standard of living, and it regards him as a "good guy" for absorbing his share, while it snickers at the prudent, self-denying, abstemious thrift that an earlier generation would have respected. In short, he has become an other-directed man. In this process it would certainly seem that economic abundance plays a more critical part than population phase in producing the transformation.

In the same way it also appears that abundance is an essential factor in creating the dilemmas which Horney regards as the characteristic causes of neuroses in the modern American personality. Here it is pertinent to recall, at the cost of repetition, the main points of Horney's analysis. She finds a constant recurrence of fears, which result from sustained hostile tension, which in turn results from a competitive outlook that extends "from the cradle to the grave." She finds, further, three dilemmas: aggressiveness grown so pronounced that it cannot be reconciled with Christian brotherhood, desire for material goods so vigorously stimulated that it cannot be satisfied, and expectations of untrammeled freedom soaring so high that they cannot be squared with the multitude of responsibilities and restrictions that confine us all.

Are not all these the results, in part at least, of our abundance and the way we use it? Increased abundance means increased rewards in the competitive struggle. Increased rewards mean an increased premium upon efficiency in competition. But what competitors can be more efficient than those who are most aggressive, most eager to reap the promised rewards, most intent upon realizing the unrestricted latitude which has been promised them? For the sake of the system, we should accentuate these qualities to the maximum, and we do accentuate them, even though aggression at its maximum violates Christian ideals; the appetite for rewards at its maximum outstrips the possibility of attaining them; and the yearning to gain complete latitude or freedom or mobility, at its maximum, clashes with the real responsibilities and limitations of life. The enticements of potential abundance tempt us to abandon the system of status, with its social bargain to trade opportunity for security, and then the absence of security sets up the anxieties which Horney regards as characteristic. If the response to the competitive stimuli is excessive, is not this because the rewards of the competitive race are inordinate? If the social pressures upon the individual to enter the competitive contest are, in some cases, literally intolerable, resulting in neurosis, is not this because society itself regards the rewards as irresistible and is determined to compel everyone to strive for them? It is a commonplace of gambling that the intentness of the players is in proportion to the size of the stakes, and the stakes of the American game have certainly contributed something toward giving it a greater tenseness than some participants can bear.

This discussion of the way in which economic surplus enters into the situations depicted by Mead, Riesman, and Horney may serve to illustrate how widely the factor of abundance may be applied in a variety of analyses. More than this, it may also contribute to showing that the analyses of these three authors are essentially homogeneous rather than disparate. If so, it is important to realize that, instead of complicating the treatment of a difficult and treacherous concept by requiring the student to choose between diverse theories, the three fall into alignment in such a way that each provides support at a different point for an integrated interpretation of the American character.

In the attempt, however, to show both the critical influence of historical determinants in shaping the culture and the vital importance of such determinants as links between history and the behavioral sciences in the study of man, it is not enough merely to pick out one determinant as a strand in these different fabrics. It is necessary to show that this determinant—in the present case, abundance—exercises a broad influence throughout the wide range of activities which make up the life of the people under investigation. The second part of this volume will therefore be devoted to a consideration of the distinctive influence which abundance has exerted upon several far-reaching aspects of the American experience. The subject is so broad that an exhaustive study would take a lifetime and would crowd a heavy volume; but, in an area where almost no systematic work has been done, even a series of samplings at various key locations in the field may serve to give at least a few new insights into the American character.

PART II

Abundance and the Shaping of American Character

Introduction to Part II

In the general discussion of the problem of national character which occupied Part I, the reader has found constant emphasis upon the significance of the work done by behavioral scientists and upon the relationship that ought to exist between these sciences and history in the study of national character. As he turns to Part II, he will find little overt attention to the behavioral position but will encounter instead a sustained consideration of a historical force, namely, economic abundance, at work in the development of American society. This apparent shift in emphasis may lead him to wonder whether the behavioral aspects are being abandoned in practice after having been established in theory.

Although the focus of immediate and overt attention does indeed shift at this point and the discussion does address itself to another aspect of the study of American character, the reciprocal contributions of history and the behavioral sciences to one another are still central to the argument. Their pertinence could be specified at almost every paragraph, but this has not been done lest it belabor the obvious. At this transition point, however, it may be in order to indicate in advance how the chapters that follow bear upon the question of what history may contribute to the behavioral analysis.

The behavioral sciences regard an awareness of the social structure, and specifically the strata of classes, as essential to their analysis of character and personality, for this structure determines the social roles which shall be assigned to every human being in the society, and the demands of the role deeply influence the character of the individual who occupies it. After the historical factor of economic abundance has been introduced in chapter iii, chapter iv considers the effect of this historical factor in producing a distinctive social structure and a distinctive mobility within the structure of American society.

The behavioral sciences properly regard the system of values which are maintained by a society as having a profound effect upon the character of individual members of the society. They also regard the distinction between an authoritarian and a voluntaristic system of relationships as being among the most critical points of difference in the conditioning of individuals. Chapter iv, dealing with the American ideal of equality, and chapter v, dealing with the American version of democracy, show how the historical factor of economic abundance has operated to produce the distinctive values and the distinctive system of voluntaristic relationships which are characteristic of the American people and which therefore impinge to some degree upon the personality of every American.

The behavioral sciences also attach importance to the individual's image of himself, and the group's image of itself, as forces in the formation of character, for the individual or the group will tend to be in fact what they imagine themselves to be in fancy. Nature holds the mirror up to art. Chapter vi is concerned with the Americans' concept of the mission of America. It discusses the large part which the historical factor of economic abundance has had in determining the mission of America, the small part which Americans have allowed to this factor in forming their self-image, and the anomalous results which have followed from the difference between the Americans as they see themselves and the Americans as others see them.

The behavioral sciences recognize that environmental forces are vital in determining the culture of any society, but they emphasize the fact that a secondary, man-made environment often supersedes the physical environment. Historians have been less conscious of this distinction. Chapter vii reviews the classic historical use of an environmental factor—the frontier—in shaping the American character, and it then analyzes the extent to which the historical factor of economic abundance may have been determinative in the frontier situation. Here the secondary environment created by abundance persisted after the primary environment of the frontier had disappeared, and, through the persistence of this secondary environment, some of the character-forming conditions which were believed to inhere only in the frontier have been perpetuated after the frontier's disappearance.

The behavioral sciences are further concerned—and very vitally concerned—with the institutions of social control. They have given close attention to the mechanisms by which society orients the individual, instructs him in his role, and imposes a set of values upon him. Here much of their attention has centered upon public institutions. Chapter viii shows how the historical factor of economic abundance has brought a new and powerful institution of social control—namely, national advertising—into being and how this institution dominates the media of public communication, sanctions a new order of values for the individual, and indoctrinates him in his role as a consumer.

Finally, chapter ix returns to the direct question of the relation between the historical determinants of character in the group sense and the cultural process of character formation in the individual sense. The study ends on this theme, for, if history and the behavioral sciences can be brought into fruitful conjunction for a more effective and more advanced study of national character, it must be in some such equation as this.

III. The Nature of American Abundance

What may be the first European description of the American standard of living appeared in the comedy, *Eastward Ho*, written in 1605 by George Chapman and John Marston. In this play one of the characters, Seagull, says of Virginia, "I tell thee, gold is more plentiful there than copper is with us. . . . Why, man, all their dripping pans are pure gold; and all their chains with which they chain up their streets are massy gold . . . and for rubies and diamonds they go forth on holidays and gather 'em by the sea-shore to hang on their children's coats."

Scapethrift asked, "And is it a pleasant country withal?" to which Seagull replied, "As ever the sun shined on: temperate and full of all sorts of excellent viands; wild boar there is as common as our tamest bacon is here, and venison as mutton."

However inaccurate this may have been in detail, it has re-mained Europe's conception of America from that day to this (even to the conviction that we spoil our children), and, though travelers have not reported the precious metals, almost all of them have emphasized the presence of wealth in other forms. Sir Thomas Dale, governor of Virginia in 1611, said of his colony: "Take foure of the best kingdomes in Christendome and put them all together, they may no way compare with this countrie either for commodities or goodnesse of soil."[1] Hector St. John de Crèvecœur, writing in the 1780's, pictured America as a land of plenty for men of every occupation and every social objec-tive: "There is room for every body in America: has he any particular talent, or industry? he exerts it in order to procure a livelihood, and it succeeds. Is he a merchant? the avenues of

1. Alexander Brown, *Genesis of the United States* (1890), I, 494.

trade are infinite; is he eminent in any respect? he will be employed and respected. Does he love a country life? pleasant farms present themselves; he may purchase what he wants, and thereby become an American farmer. Is he a labourer, sober and industrious? he need not go many miles, nor receive many informations before he will be hired, well fed at the table of his employer, and paid four or five times more than he can get in Europe. Does he want uncultivated lands? thousands of acres present themselves, which he may purchase cheap. Whatever be his talents or inclinations, if they are moderate, he may satisfy them. I do not mean, that every one who comes will grow rich in a little time; no, but he may procure an easy, decent maintenance, by his industry. Instead of starving, he will be fed; instead of being idle, he will have employment; and these are riches enough for such men as come over here."[2] Commenting on the American dietary, William Cobbett in 1817 observed that "you are not much pressed to eat and drink, but such an abundance is spread before you . . . that you instantly lose all restraint."[3] Alexis de Tocqueville spoke of the valley of the Mississippi as "the most magnificent dwelling place prepared by God for man's abode," and he remarked that fortune offered "an immense booty to the Americans."

Such quotations could be multiplied almost to infinity and could be projected down to the most recent moment of American history. Without attempting to pillage this morning's newspaper for examples, it is interesting to note one or two fairly recent expressions. Henry Bamford Parkes, in *The American Experience*, speaks of the "unexampled abundance of land and resources" as "the cardinal factor in the development of American civilization."[4] Chester Wilmot made an interesting indirect

2. Quoted in Henry Steele Commager, *America in Perspective: The United States through Foreign Eyes* (New York: Mentor Books, 1948), pp. 28–29.

3. *Ibid.*, p. xii. 4. (New York: Alfred A. Knopf, 1947), p. 8.

allusion to this same factor in *The Struggle for Europe* (1952), when he pointed out as a distinctive characteristic of the American Army that it tends to concentrate upon development of its own strength and, unlike the British army, does not normally seek victory by playing upon its opponent's weaknesses. Only a clear superiority of resources, of course, would warrant such policy. Even more striking is the reported assertion of Franklin D. Roosevelt that, if he could place one American book in the hands of every Russian, the volume of his choice would be a Sears, Roebuck catalogue.

Throughout our national experience, the most varied types of observers have agreed in emphasizing America's bounty. Explorers have marveled at wealth previously undiscovered; travelers have contrasted the riches of America with the scarcity of the lands from which they came; millions of inhabitants of the Old World have responded as immigrants to the lure of the land of plenty, the land of promise, where they could "dwell like kings in fairyland, lords of the soil"; politicians have urged the voter to vote himself a farm or a check for thirty dollars every Thursday or an old age pension or a war bonus, in the confident assurance that the country can meet the draft;[5] exploiters have parried demands for conservation by contending that the sources of our wealth are unlimited; a whole battalion of statisticians has been deployed on the task of measuring the abundance of natural resources—our cultivable soil, our hydroelectric potential, our timber, our coal, our iron, our copper, our petroleum, our natural gas, and so on; while another battalion has concentrated upon showing how the potential wealth of natural resources has been translated into an unexampled standard of living.

5. The following pioneer song is quoted in Eric F. Goldman, *Rendezvous with Destiny* (New York: Alfred A. Knopf, 1953), p. 27:

"Come along, come along, make no delay,
Come from every nation, come from every way,
Our lands are broad enough, don't be alarmed,
For Uncle Sam is rich enough to give us all a farm."

In every aspect of economic welfare the national differentials between the United States and other countries are immense, and some of these differentials, which have been conveniently summarized by Karl W. Deutsch, are illustrated in Figures 1 and 2.[6] Figure 1 shows that the wages per hour of unskilled laborers in the United States, Canada, and New Zealand, for the year 1940, were about 60 per cent greater than the wages of

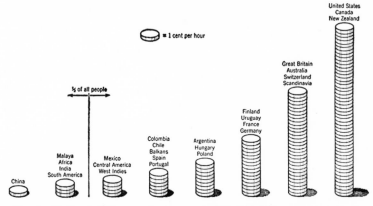

FIG. 1.—National differences in the wages of unskilled laborers, 1940 (various occupations), according to Erwin Raisz, using data from the *International Labour Review*, 1941. (From *Atlas of Global Geography* [New York: Global Press and Harper & Bros., 1944], p. 49. Reproduced by permission.)

similar workers in such advanced countries as Great Britain, Australia, and Switzerland and about 400 per cent greater than wages in most of Latin America. Figure 2 shows, by the height of the blocks, per capita incomes in seventy countries in 1949, in dollars of 1949 purchasing power. It shows that per capita income

6. Karl W. Deutsch, *Nationalism and Social Communication* (Boston: Technology Press of the Massachusetts Institute of Technology; New York: John Wiley & Sons, Inc., 1953), pp. 36–45. Figs. 1 and 2 are taken from Deutsch, pp. 36, 40, but the original source for Fig. 1 is *Atlas of Global Geography* (New York: Global Press and Harper & Bros., 1944), p. 49; and for Fig. 2, *National and Per Capita Incomes of Seventy Countries* ("United Nations Statistical Papers," ser. E, No. 1 [October, 1950]), Table 1, pp. 14–16.

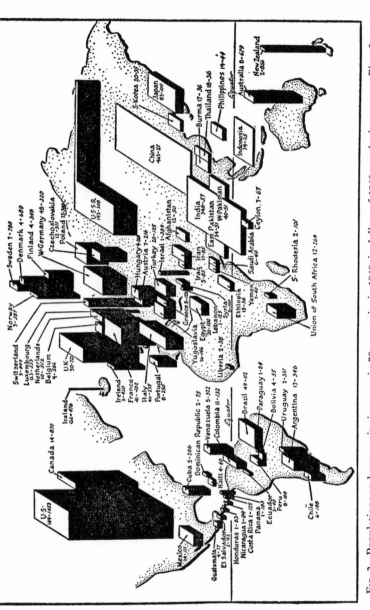

Fig. 2.—Populations and per capita incomes in 70 countries in 1949, in dollars of 1949 purchasing power. *First figure*: Population in millions of people, represented by area of white rectangles. *Second figure*: Per capita income in 1949 dollars, represented by height of blocks. National income is represented by volume of each block. Data from *National and Per Capita Incomes of Seventy Countries* ("United Nations Statistical Papers," ser. E, No. 1 [Lake Success: Statistical Office of the United Nations, 1950]), pp. 14–16.

for the United States was $1,453, with no other country exceeding $900. Canada, New Zealand, and Switzerland were in the $800–$900 range; Sweden and the United Kingdom at the $700–$800 level; and no others exceeded $700. That is, no others reached a level half as high as that of the United States. The figure for the Soviet Union was $308. Argentina's $346 was the highest in Latin America, and Haiti's and Ecuador's $40 were the lowest, while the lowest world figure was for China, with a per capita income of $21 per year, or $1.75 per month.

Other data, cited by Deutsch, show that the United States, with 7 per cent of the world's population, has 42 per cent of the world's income, which means that a world population about fourteen times as great as that of the United States enjoys a collective income which is only 38 per cent greater than the income of the United States.

We may measure this differential in the human terms of nourishment rather than in the economic terms of income. In 1949 reliable computations showed that the average American consumed 3,186 calories daily. This was unquestionably the highest nutritional standard in the world. The consumption in England was estimated at more than 2,700, but in France, Italy, and Western Germany it was between 2,201 and 2,700. In Algeria, the Philippines, Japan, and India in the Old World, as well as in El Salvador in the New, it was below 1,800. It obviously must be a factor of immense importance in the daily lives of people that some habitually have more than enough to eat, while others are habitually hungry, and students of personality who regard relations within the family and practices of infant training as critical might surely find in these data a stunning opportunity to apply Gerth and Mills's proposition that "the structural and historical features of modern society must be connected with the most intimate features of man's self."

The compilation of statistics might be extended endlessly, but it would only prove repetitively that in every aspect of material plenty America possesses unprecedented riches and that these are very widely distributed among one hundred and fifty million American people. If few can cite the figures, everyone knows that we have, per capita, more automobiles, more telephones, more radios, more vacuum cleaners, more electric lights, more bathtubs, more supermarkets and movie palaces and hospitals, than any other nation. Even at mid-century prices we can afford college educations and T-bone steaks for a far higher proportion of our people than receive them anywhere else on the globe.

It approaches the commonplace, then, to observe that the factor of relative abundance is, by general consent, a basic condition of American life. As to the fact itself, we have demonstrated it in a thousand measurements of our own plenty. But it may be that we have emphasized this too much as an economic fact and not enough as a social one—that we have not sufficiently considered the pervasive influence of abundance upon many aspects of our lives which have no obvious relation to the standard of living. For certainly it is an influence that impinges upon all American social conditions and contributes in the most fundamental way to the shaping of the American culture and the American character.

Before considering its influence, however, we might do well to examine the nature of this abundance. A vital distinction separates mere potential abundance—the copious supply of natural resources—and actual abundance—the availability to society of a generous quota of goods ready for use. The two are not unrelated, of course, for a generous physical endowment is essential to any country in providing the raw materials from which the supply of goods is produced, or at least one might suppose it to be essential if Great Britain had not been, for a century, the richest country on the planet, although not the site of any of nature's major stores of resources. But to say that physical plenty is conducive to social plenty—that the potential precedes the actual— is not at all the same as to say that every potentiality will become an actuality or even that the growing actuality will remain within the limits indicated by the potentiality from which it sprang. This is illustrated even within the United States by the fact that New England, which, among the regions, is nature's stepchild, maintained for a long time a standard of living as high as, or higher than, that of any other part of the country.

Social wealth, as contrasted with natural wealth, results not only from the supply of resources but also from a nation's systems of production and distribution. Without elaboration on this point, it may be worth while to mention that Colin Clark, in his *Conditions of Economic Progress* (London: Macmillan & Co., 1940), shows that at different phases of economic development the proportion of the socially useful output from the productive system varies considerably, and he argues that these phases require analysis if the causes of great difference in world income are to be explained; glib reference to natural resources, he says, is not enough. To appreciate the full truth of this assertion, it is, perhaps, necessary only to remember that the American Indians possessed, but benefited little from, the fertile soil which formed an unprecedented source of wealth for the colonists; that the colonists gained little more than the grinding of their grain from the water power which made magnates of the early industrialists; that the early industrialists set little store by the deposits of petroleum and ore which served as a basis for the fortunes of the post–Civil War period; that the industrial captains of the late nineteenth century had no conception of the values that lay latent in water power as a force for generating electricity, which would be developed by the enterprisers of the twentieth century; and that these early twentieth-century enterprisers were as little able to capitalize the values of uranium as the Indians had been five centuries earlier. The social value of natural resources depends entirely upon the aptitude of society for using them.[7]

7. Isaiah Bowman has stated the distinction between the physical resources and the physical capacity of a land as follows: "Man himself is . . . a part of

The importance of human resourcefulness in developing the value of natural resources is worth emphasizing, for critics of this country have often dismissed the American standard of living as an example of luck *in excelsis*. They repeat the saying that there is a special providence which watches over drunkards, fools, and the United States, and they interpret the prosperity of this country as a simple reflex of nature's profusion. As they see it, the Americans are a people who have wandered unwittingly into a vast cornucopia whose plenty is accepted with moronic complacency.

Of course, no one ought to minimize the bountiful good fortune which has befallen the American people; but is it not too simple merely to picture the American as the lucky winner of nature's lottery? In other parts of the world other peoples have eked out a meager existence amid natural resources which were technologically meaningless to them and yet were comparable to the resources of North America. In some places there are people who still do this today. The working economic assets of a society depend not only upon the supply of natural resources but also upon the effectiveness with which resources are converted into energy or productive capacity or goods and even upon the use which is made of these goods in exchange.

But this effectiveness in the conversion of resources is not a matter of largesse or luck. It is determined by the economic organization and the technological advancement of any given society, and these factors are the result of human endeavor and

his own environment; his skill and knowledge are assets to him as definitely as that which nature provides in the raw. We cannot determine the capacity of a land from its physical aspects alone, its soil, its water supply, its temperature means and extremes, its forests, or the presence or absence of fisheries and the like. Greenland was one kind of country to the Vikings; it was another kind of country to the Eskimos; it would be still another kind of country to us. . . . Its *capacity* or potential would vary widely in these three cases" ("Geography in the Creative Experience," *Geographical Review,* XXVIII [1937], 11).

achievement and of other factors besides physical endowment. One might suppose that the study of economics would long ago have subjected these factors and all the determinants of economic growth to detailed analysis and that such analysis would now provide a means of evaluating the relative weight which should be given to natural resources, on the one hand, and to human initiative, on the other, in the production of an economy of plenty. But, surprisingly enough, economists have only recently begun to address themselves to this problem. The National Bureau of Economic Research in 1949 published a volume of papers on *Problems in the Study of Economic Growth,* to which John Maurice Clark contributed a discussion of "Common and Disparate Elements in National Growth and Decline." Clark listed a sequence of "conditioning factors" which he regarded as critical to the determination of economic growth. The first of these was "climate and natural resources," but he remarked that it is "commonplace . . . that natural resources are relative to a people's capacity to use them." His second factor was "quality of population," in connection with which he argued the importance of education, of moral qualities, and of "diffused ingenuity and enterprise." Third, he discussed "incentives," and here he observed that "the great volume of economic growth has come under . . . individualistic incentives." His fourth factor was "capital," and his final one was "institutional conditions and systems." Here, again, he spoke of the importance of individualism and observed that "different kinds of growth are favored by different kinds of institutional frameworks. It is difficult to see how the exuberant expansion of this country in the nineteenth century could have been brought about under anything but an individualistic system."

The only other important study in this field is Walt W. Rostow's *The Process of Economic Growth* (New York: W. W. Norton & Co., 1952). Rostow observes the fact that economists have hesitated to take account of any but the most narrowly economic factors in explaining economic growth; but he believes that the subject should be studied within a framework of the human or social propensities which "summarize the effective response of a society to its environment at any given period of time." These impulses or lines of activity are the propensities to develop fundamental science, to apply science to economic ends, to accept innovations, to seek material advance, to consume, and to have children.

It is not a part of this inquiry to attempt an evaluation of the ideas of either Clark or Rostow. The point is simply that both these eminent economists reduce the factor of environmental riches to a relatively small place in the explanation of economic growth. Both place heavy emphasis upon factors of human ingenuity, human initiative, human adaptability, and human enterprise. In fact, they seem not far from accepting a more refined equivalent of the old, popular assertion that determination, ingenuity, and hard work made America what it is. Clark is apparently aware how closely he approaches this position, for he cautions that, although he believes that the individualistic system paced the growth of American wealth, he also believes that "a strongly-individualistic system will ultimately encounter decline unless its individualism is balanced by controls to conserve essential social assets, including the imponderable asset which centers in the individual's sense of a stake in a community which can be trusted to treat him as a member of a community should be treated, taking care and responsibility for his access to opportunity, and for his fate if major calamity strikes."

Clearly, however, this volume has already undertaken enough, without attempting to bring in a verdict on the free-enterprise system. The only point to be established here is that expert opinion regards the qualities of a people and the techniques and institutions of a society as vital factors in the process of economic growth. The qualities which are regarded as important are initiative and capacity for productive work, and thus the conclusion is indicated that human enterprise, quite as much as the bounty of nature, has been vital in supplying the flow of usable goods which constitute American abundance.

On this important point, two illustrations may suffice. First, it is a social fact of incalculable importance that between 1820 and 1930, by exploiting new sources of power, America increased forty fold the supply of energy which it could command per capita. This was, in effect, a forty-fold increase in capacity to convert and utilize resources, and it was achieved not merely by accepting nature's proffered gifts but by the application of science, by the elaboration of a complex economic organization, by planning, and by toil. Second, it is a scarcely less important fact that the United States has so improved the technology of food production that, while in 1820 we were obliged to keep 71.8 per cent of our working population engaged in agriculture in order to feed the rest, today (in 1950) 11.6 per cent of our working population engaged in agriculture can feed themselves and the remaining 88.4 per cent as well. If the proportions of 1820 still prevailed, it would require more than 46,000,000 of our labor force of 64,000,000 to provide food, and we would have to divert 39,800,000 workers from other activities to perform this function. From these data it is strikingly evident that the extraordinary productivity of American agriculture could never have been achieved by the availability of fertile soil alone, even in infinite amount; it was accomplished by the specialization of labor, by scientific agriculture, and most of all by the mechanization of farm operations. Thus it is safe to say that the American standard of living is a resultant much less of natural resources than of the increase in capacity to produce and that this was the result, directly, of human endeavor—the ventures and struggles of the pioneer, the exertions of the workman, the ingenuity of the inventor, the drive of the enterpriser, and the economic efficiency of all kinds of Americans, who shared a notorious addiction to hard work. These activities may themselves be the product of deterministic forces, and no implication of superior merit is necessarily involved; but, at least, one important point emerges—namely, that American abundance is a condition which has been achieved in the same way that other goals have been achieved by other men at other times throughout history, and it is not a mere matter of getting into the path of blind luck. Though based upon a primary environment, abundance is realized through the creation by society of a secondary environment, and it should be regarded accordingly.

But, though the nature and causes of American abundance may have been misunderstood, the importance of it has never been doubted, and a long procession of travelers, other observers, and social analysts have pointed to it as a basic and conspicuous feature of American life. Accepting it as such, I attempted in chapter ii to show its applicability to three recent interpretations of the American character by behavioral scientists. The chapters which follow are concerned with its effect, as a historical force, upon some of America's distinctive ideals, institutions, and social practices.

IV. Abundance, Mobility, and Status

Abundance has influenced American life in many ways, but there is perhaps no respect in which this influence has been more profound than in the forming and strengthening of the American ideal and practice of equality, with all that the ideal has implied for the individual in the way of opportunity to make his own place in society and of emancipation from a system of status.

The very meaning of the term "equality" reflects this influence, for the connotations to an American are quite unlike what they might be to a European. A European, advocating equality, might very well mean that all men should occupy positions that are on roughly the same level in wealth, power, or enviability. But the American, with his emphasis upon equality of opportunity, has never conceived of it in this sense. He has traditionally expected to find a gamut ranging from rags to riches, from tramps to millionaires.[1] To call this "equality" may seem a contradiction in terms, but the paradox has been resolved in two ways: first, by declaring that all men are equal in the eyes of the law—an explanation which, by itself, could have satisfied only the more legalistic type of mind; and, second, by assuming that no man is restricted or confined by his status to any one station, or even to any maximum station. Thus equality did not mean uniform position on a common level, but it did mean universal opportunity to move through a scale which traversed many levels. At one end

1. The European annoyance at the way in which Americans use the term "equality" is suggested in G. Lowes Dickinson, *A Modern Symposium* (1905), where he speaks of the American policy of "indistinction,": "Indistinction, I say, rather than equality, for the word equality is misleading, and might seem to imply, for example, a social and economic parity of conditions, which no more exists in America than it does in Europe" (p. 96).

of the scale might stand a log cabin, at the other the White House; but equality meant that anyone might run the entire scale. This emphasis upon unrestricted latitude as the essence of equality in turn involved a heavy emphasis upon liberty as an essential means for keeping the scale open and hence making equality a reality as well as a theoretical condition. In other societies, liberty—the principle that allows the individual to be different from others—might seem inconsistent with equality—the principle that requires the individual to be similar to others; but in America "liberty," meaning "freedom to grasp opportunity," and "equality," also meaning "freedom to grasp opportunity," have become almost synonymous.[2]

In short, equality came to mean, in a major sense, parity in competition. Its value was as a means to advancement rather than as an asset in itself. Like an option in the world of business, it had no intrinsic value but only a value when used. Since the potential value could be realized only by actual movement to a higher level, the term "equality" acquired for most Americans exactly the same connotations which the term "upward mobility" has for the social scientist.

Understanding equality or mobility in this way, one can readily see the effect of abundance upon it. Alexis de Tocqueville perceived the relationship very clearly and stated it forcibly when he observed that "the chief circumstance which has favored the establishment and the maintenance of a democratic system in the United States is the nature of the territory that the Americans inhabit. Their ancestors gave them the love of equality and of freedom; but God Himself gave them the means of remaining equal and free by placing them upon a boundless continent." Clearly, Tocqueville did not really mean that the Americans needed a boundless continent to assure them of equality in the

2. "The bourgeois found in the concept of equality a ladder to climb on" (David Riesman, "Equality and Social Structure," *Journal of Legal and Political Sociology*, I [1942], 74).

sense of being on a common level. He meant that a boundless continent enabled them to fulfil the promise of mobility. Democracy made this promise, but the riches of North America fulfilled it; and our democratic system, which, like other systems, can survive only when its ideals are realized, survived because an economic surplus was available to pay democracy's promissory notes.

Throughout our history the development of new geographical areas and new segments of the economy has offered those instances of advancement to which we point when offering illustrative proof that our system of equality enables anyone to succeed. What we mean, more nearly, is that our system of equality removes certain negative impediments to success, and then our positive access to a larger measure of abundance permits fulfilment of the success promise.

The point may seem self-evident when stated, but it is a fact which we have consistently and effectively suppressed in the national consciousness. Thus during the Depression, when economic access to advancement was lacking, men nevertheless tended to blame themselves as guilty in failing to achieve it, for they still had their freedom from legal restraints, and they had been taught to believe that this was all that they needed. As long as they continued to enjoy exemption from the negative impediments, the set of their mind was such that they did not recognize that the exemption had no meaning except in conjunction with positive opportunity.

Today our somewhat disillusioned intellectuals tend to emphasize the fact that the American dream of absolute equality and of universal opportunity was never fulfilled in the literal sense, and they often play up the discrepancy between the realities of American life and the beliefs of the American creed. Discrepancy there is, was, and perhaps ever shall be, and it must be confronted in any analysis; but the recognition of it should not obscure another primary fact, namely, that American conditions, in addition to encouraging a belief in mobility, actually brought about a condition of mobility far more widespread and pervasive than any previous society or previous era of history had ever witnessed.

The classic illustration, always cited in this connection, is the frontier, and it is indeed true that the existence of the frontier presented people with a unique opportunity to put behind them the economic and social status which they held in their native communities and to acquire property and standing in the newly forming communities of the West. But, while we constantly remind ourselves that the West offered abundance in the form of free land and provided the frontier as a locus for the transformation of this abundance into mobility, we often forget that the country as a whole offered abundance in the form of fuel resources, mineral resources, bumper crops, industrial capacity, and the like, and provided the city as a locus for the transformation of this abundance into mobility. More Americans have changed their status by moving to the city than have done so by moving to the frontier. The urban migration is almost as great a factor in American development as the westward migration, and more young men have probably followed Horace Greeley's example in moving from a rural birthplace to a metropolis than have followed his precept to go west and grow up with the country.

In America, the processes of an expanding economy—expanding geographically to open new territorial areas, expanding technologically to open new realms of production—have provided a constant supply of advantageous positions to which enterprising people could advance from less favored beginnings and have also provided, until 1921, a steady flow of immigrants to insure that the lower economic ranks need not be left empty by the ceaseless trend upward. Each wave of immigrants, in turn, was likely to move up as succeeding waves came in at the bottom. If opportunity, operating from above, has exerted a drawing force, pulling individuals upward, immigration, operating from below, has exerted a thrusting force, pushing them upward. But it is the factor of abundance, like the steam alternately generated and condensed in an engine, which has simultaneously exerted the force of drawing and that of thrusting.

There is a real question how much of the rapid transformation of America has been marked by actual mobility in the sense of advancement by the individual through the ranks of society from one status to another and how much has been a mere change in the manner of life and standard of living of classes which retain pretty much the same relative position. The middle-class city dweller of today has a money income that would have connoted wealth to his frugal, landowning, farm-dwelling forebear of the nineteenth century, and his facilities for living make his forebear's life seem Spartan by comparison; but his standing in the community is no higher and is, in fact, considerably less independent. Improvements in the standard of living of society at large should not be confused with the achievement of separate social advancement by individuals.

But even allowing for this distinction, it bears repeating that America has had a greater measure of social equality and social mobility than any highly developed society in human history. In terms of geographical movement ("horizontal mobility," as it is sometimes called), it has been characteristically American for the individual to make his life in a place distant from his family home, which is to say that he achieves his own status instead of receiving one which is entailed upon him. In terms of economic and social ups and downs ("vertical mobility," so called) America has been the country where the cycle "from shirtsleeves to shirtsleeves" was three generations, which is to say that status has changed readily and rapidly. In America, education has been more available to people with native ability; professional and business opportunities have been more available to people with education; wealth has been more available to people who excelled in business and the professions; and social fortresses have yielded to the assaults of wealth more readily than in any other country. At every stage, the channels of mobility have been kept open. As for social distinctions, certainly they exist; but, whatever their power may be, social rank can seldom assert an open claim to deference in this country, and it usually makes at least a pretense of conformity to equalitarian ways. Certain conspicuous exceptions, such as the treatment of American Negroes, qualify all these assertions but do not invalidate them as generalizations.

Americans have attached immense value, of course, to this condition of equal opportunity. It has, they feel, enabled men and women in this country, more than anywhere else in the world, to find, develop, and exercise their best potentialities as human beings. Such opportunity has not only meant fulfilment for the individual; it has also been of great value to society: it has enabled the nation to make the optimum use of its human resources by recruiting talent from the whole body of the population and not merely from a limited class, and thus it has strengthened the arts, the sciences, the economic enterprise, and the government of the country.

Moreover, American society, as a society of abundance, especially needed men who would accept the challenge of mobility. Historically, as new lands, new forms of wealth, new opportunities, came into play, clamoring to be seized upon, America developed something of a compulsion to make use of them.[3] The man best qualified for this role was the completely mobile man, moving freely from one locality to the next, from one economic position to another, or from one social level to levels above. The

3. "The real end which Americans set before themselves is Acceleration. To be always moving, and always moving faster, that they think is the beatific life. . . . Hence, their contempt for the leisure so much valued by Europeans. Leisure they feel to be a kind of standing still, the unpardonable sin" (G. Lowes Dickinson, *op. cit.*, pp. 104–5).

rapidity of economic change required a high degree of convertibility, of transmutability, in the economic elements which it employed, and the system of mobility imparted this necessary flexibility in the human resources which were needed. In a country where the entire environment was to be transformed with the least possible delay, a man who was not prepared to undergo personal transformation was hardly an asset. Hence mobility became not merely an optional privilege but almost a mandatory obligation, and the man who failed to meet this obligation had, to a certain extent, defaulted in his duty to society.

Because of these values and these compulsions, America not only practiced a full measure of mobility and social equality but also developed a creed of equality and articulated a myth to accompany the creed.

The myth of equality held that equality exists not merely as a potentiality in the nature of man but as a working actuality in the operation of American society—that advantages or handicaps are not really decisive and that every man is the architect of his own destiny. It asserted the existence in the United States of a classless society, where no one is better than anyone else and merit is the only recognized ground of distinction. Despite their patent implausibility, these ideas received and still retain a most tenacious hold. Americans are notoriously unresponsive to the concept of class warfare, and American workers, while fully alert to the protection of their economic interests, have never accepted identity as members of a working class in the way in which workers in England and other countries have. As Margaret Mead observes, "the assumption that men were created equal, with an equal ability to make an effort and win an earthly reward, although denied every day by experience, is maintained every day by our folklore and our day dreams." American fondness for the underdog is perhaps not so much a matter of sympathy for causes which are losing (America cares little for causes which are lost) as of desire to see the creed of equality proved by the success of those who appear less than equal.[4]

So long as these beliefs can be maintained intact—so long as they approximate reality closely enough to be convincing—they exercise an immense moral power. From them are derived many of the attitudes that make for decency in American life. The optimism with which Americans have confronted the future; the confidence with which they have grappled with difficult problems; their conviction that merit will be rewarded and that honest work is the only reliable means to attain success; their integrity in social relations; and their respect for the human dignity of any man or woman, regardless of that person's social credentials, are

4. Note the following comment that appeared in the Hartford *Courant*, August 28, 1950, on the outcome of the United States Amateur golf championship contest:

"SOMETHING THE RUSSIANS WOULDN'T UNDERSTAND

"Wonder if the Russians understand the story that appeared in Sunday's sport sections concerning the final of the United States Amateur golf championship?

"Seems that the son of a very rich man [Frank Stranahan] played the son of a poor man [Sam Urzetta] in the final. The rich man's son has been devoting his life to the improvement of his golf game. He has played winter and summer circuit, both here and abroad, studied under the best teachers available. The poor man's son—his father is a janitor—hasn't been around much. The only title he owned up to Saturday night was the New York State Amateur. He has never played in England or Scotland and probably he has never played in Florida or California. But the janitor's son beat the rich man's son and won the United States Amateur golf championship. The Russians must find it hard to reconcile this with their zany notions of how things happen in a democracy. The stories late Saturday night on the news service wires said Sam Urzetta's sister, a meat market clerk in East Rochester, had 'gone crazy' trying to keep her mind on her work while her brother was winning the amateur golf championship of the United States. The stories also said that Sam's mother, Mrs. Carmen Urzetta, had been praying for two days at a little shrine in her bedroom. The Russians wouldn't understand these things, either."

It is notable that the account does not indicate what interest, if any, Mr. Stranahan's mother took in the contest or whether she sought to invoke divine aid.

all by-products of the ideal of full equality in a classless society. But, with all its value, this ideal has never been maintained without a certain cost, for it breeds great expectations, and, in so far as these expectations fail of realization, social and personal tensions result. As we move past the mid-point of the twentieth century, it is becoming increasingly clear that the ideal confronts two serious and growing difficulties. One of these difficulties is that we really cannot attain a classless society, and the other is that we have sacrificed some very valuable qualities of the now repudiated status system in an effort to attain it.

Belief in a classless society in the literal sense was an illusion from the beginning, for, as Pitirim A. Sorokin has remarked, "unstratified society with real equality of its members is a myth which has never been realized in the history of mankind. . . . The forms and proportions of stratification may vary, but its essence is permanent." But Sorokin also mentions that a large measure of mobility will produce the illusion that there are no strata, and America has apparently had in the past more than enough mobility to sustain the illusion.[5] Today the degree of mobility is apparently somewhat reduced, and a growing awareness of the invisible barriers of social class has resulted.

The existence of social class in this sense has been fully demonstrated by a number of intensive social studies which analyze the structure of the American system of social hierarchy and which seek to define its strata in precise terms. The foremost of these in exhaustiveness of investigation is W. Lloyd Warner's analysis of a New England coastal town, in the "Yankee City" volumes which began to be published eleven years ago, but there are several others, including Warner's own survey of "Jonesville," a middle western community; August de B. Hollingshead's analysis of

5. An imaginary speaker in G. Lowes Dickinson's *A Modern Symposium* says, "I prefer a society where people have places and know them. They always do have places in any possible society; only in a democratic society they refuse to recognize them" (p. 8).

the youth of "Elmtown"—the same middle western town; Davis, Gardner, and Gardner's investigation of a southern community in their volume, *Deep South;* Robert and Helen Lynd's two volumes on *Middletown;* and James West's *Plainville, U.S.A.*; not to mention John Dollard's *Caste and Class in a Southern Town,* published in 1937. In some respects, these studies remain controversial: for instance, disagreement prevails as to whether the so-called "classes" are objective, self-conscious social groupings or whether they are mere classificatory devices for the investigator. To state it in another way, there is a lively dispute as to whether social distinctions are aligned along an unbroken gradient from the top to the bottom of society or whether they shape society into a number of levels, like stair steps. But, in any case, the studies all demonstrate abundantly that social inequalities prevail and that these inequalities can be correlated with factors such as occupation, income, education, and area of residence and can be verified by various statistical procedures. One characteristic of these strata, quite generally recognized, is that the bulk of the population falls within the middle class and another large group within the upper zone of the lower class. For instance, the middle classes of "Yankee City" and "Jonesville" contain 38 and 42 per cent of the population, respectively, while the upper-lower group accounts for 28 and 41 per cent, respectively. Another tendency which seems evident, though it cannot be verified by any such clear-cut enumeration, is that the ease of mobility from class to class appears to be diminishing, and the barriers between classes are growing increasingly difficult to pass.

The existence of social strata in America is, to repeat, in no sense unique, for such strata have existed in every advanced society, and society has always accommodated itself to them. But, though class divisions are nothing new, there are certain elements in the stratification of today which set it apart from earlier class stratification and which make the American situation essentially unique.

One of these elements is the fact that social barriers in this country are a violation of our national ideals, and therefore the mere awareness of them impairs public morale. Whereas other societies accept them as part of the order of nature, we have refused to recognize them and have conducted life on the theory that they do not exist. Hence our people are not prepared to encounter them and are less able psychologically to adjust to them, with the result that, when such barriers do force themselves upon public notice, many people either lose confidence in themselves or rebel against the society which, as they feel, betrayed them with a false promise. In America some of the ripest recruits for Marxism have been the idealists who loved the doctrine of equality too well and who would not compromise with the realities of a society which merely offered a relatively closer approach to equality than other stratified societies afford. But the problem created by social rebels is less serious than the problem of men and women who are personally broken and defeated by a system which sets one standard for what people shall attempt and another for what they may attain. Thus there was much point in certain questions posed by Margaret Mead in 1942: "Has the American scene shifted so that we still demand of every child a measure of success which is actually less and less possible for him to attain? . . . Have we made it a condition of success that a man should reach a position higher than his father's when such an achievement (for the many) is dependent upon the existence of a frontier and an expanding economy?"[6]

This conflict between the ideal and the actuality, which is one of the peculiarly American aspects of social stratification, has been clearly recognized by all students of the subject; but there is another aspect which has been generally overlooked, though it is of marked importance. This is the fact that American social distinctions, however real they may be and however difficult to

6. *And Keep Your Powder Dry* (New York: William Morrow & Co., 1942), pp. 68–69.

break down, are not based upon or supported by great disparities in wealth, in education, in speech, in dress, etc., as they are in the Old World. If the American class structure is in reality very unlike the classless society which we imagine, it is equally unlike the formalized class societies of former times, and thus it should be regarded as a new kind of social structure in which the strata may be fully demarked but where the bases of demarcation are relatively intangible. The factor of abundance has exercised a vital influence in producing this kind of structure, for it has constantly operated to equalize the overt differences between the various classes and to eliminate the physical distance between them, without, however, destroying the barriers which separate them. The traditional dissimilarities in social demeanor, in education, in dress, and in recreation made class distinction in the past seem natural and perhaps, in a pragmatic sense, justifiable, while the social chasm between, for instance, an upper class which attended school and a lower class which did not diminished the element of what might be called "invidious proximity." Where extremes of wealth and poverty, education and ignorance, privilege and exploitation prevail, resentment is directed against these conditions themselves and not against class distinctions, which are a mere recognition of the conditions. If the poor, the hungry, the ragged, the unlettered man complains, his complaint is not that he is excluded from select society, in his starved, ill-clad, ignorant condition; it is rather that he is denied decent food, decent garments, and a chance to learn. But when, living in a society that practices outward uniformity, he gains a satisfactory income, acquires education, dresses himself and his wife in the standard clothes worn by all the members of the community, sends his children to school —and then finds himself the object of class discriminations imposed at close quarters and based upon marginal, tenuous criteria, which are, in any case, probably invisible to his eyes, then the system of classes itself, no longer natural, no longer inevitable, begins to seem unjust and hateful.

If this analysis is accurate, it means that abundance has brought about an entirely new sort of inequality. By diminishing the physical differentials, the social diversity, and the real economic disparities that once separated classes, it has made any class distinction or class stratification seem doubly unfair and discriminatory. In proportion as it has solved the problem of class differentials, it has accentuated the problem of class distinctions.

Thus the goal of social equality in a classless society, which abundance seemed to make possible and which the mobility drive promised to achieve, has been sought at a substantial cost. By presenting an unattainable ideal as if it were a reality, the mobility drive has created damaging psychological tensions; by eliminating class diversity without being able to abolish class distinctions, abundance has only made subjective discrimination more galling, while making objective differentials less evident. But, in addition to these costs, the quest for equality has exacted a still more serious price: while it could not fulfil its promise to create a classless society, it has destroyed the one value which seemed inherent in the traditional class society—namely, that sense of the organic, recognized relationship between the individual and the community which was defined by the individual's status. To speak of our social structure today as a "status system," which Warner does, seems in some ways a perversion of the original term, for the actual effect of our system is to deny assured status to all except the members of the top class. Status, truly understood, implies a condition of corporate membership in the group and thus a sense of belonging in the community. It implies also a condition of dependence by the group upon the individual for the performance of certain specific work and thus makes possible a sense of worth for the individual and a pride in performance, no matter how humble his labor. The principle of true status assures the individual that he may lead a meritorious and respected life in the station where circumstances have placed him, regardless of what that station may be. Peter Drucker describes the values of status eloquently but without exaggeration when he says: "Social status and function are terms of relationship, of 'belonging,' of identification, of harmony. 'Status' defines man's existence as related in mutual necessity to the organized group. 'Function' ties his work, his aspirations and ambitions to the power and purposes of the organized group in a bond that satisfies both individual and society. . . . Together, status and function resolve the apparently irresolvable conflict between the absolute claim of the group—before which any one man is nothing in himself and only a member of the species—and the absolute claim of the individual, to whom the group is only a means and a tool for the achievement of his own private purpose. . . . Without . . . [status], man is either the 'caged spirit' of Oriental philosophy, senselessly and meaninglessly caught in a senseless and meaningless life, or just 'Homo Sapiens' and one of the . . . brutish apes. But the group's own cohesion and survival also depend on the individual's status and function; without it, the group is a mere herd, never a society."[7]

In America, of course, status, as fixed differential social position, has long been in disrepute. Ever since the Revolutionary War, it has borne the hateful implications of privilege and subservience; it connoted the attitude of English common folk who were supposed to pray,

> "God bless the squire and his relations,
> And keep us in our proper stations."

Thus status incurred obloquy, and even the party of conservatism—that is, the Republican party—rejected it. Probably nothing has contributed more to the weakness of the conservative position in the United States than the fact that this principle, which the great conservative leaders like Edmund Burke and Benjamin Dis-

7. *The New Society: The Anatomy of the Industrial Order* (New York: Harper & Bros., 1949), pp. 151–54. For an excellent appraisal of the importance of status in this sense see Robert A. Nisbet, *The Quest for Community* (New York: Oxford University Press, 1953).

raeli have recognized as the foundation stone of conservatism, has been so sharply rejected by American conservatives that it fell by default to the opposition. Ultimately, Franklin Roosevelt did more to give men a sense of status than all the Republican Presidents since Lincoln.[8]

The heavy emphasis which America has placed upon mobility of course necessitated this rejection of status, for the two are basically contradictory. Whereas the principle of status affirms that a minor position may be worthy, the principle of mobility, as Americans have construed it, regards such a station both as the penalty for and the proof of personal failure. This view is often pushed to a point where even the least invidious form of subordination comes to be resented as carrying a stigma, and certain kinds of work which are socially necessary are almost never performed except grudgingly. The individual, driven by the belief that he should never rest content in his existing station and knowing that society demands advancement by him as proof of his merit, often feels stress and insecurity and is left with no sense of belonging either in the station to which he advances or in the one from which he set out.

After nearly two hundred years, these difficulties now begin to be recognized, and there is a dawning realization that both our

8. Justice William O. Douglas, speaking on Roosevelt on May 30, 1948, said: "The sense of belonging is important to man. The feeling that he is accepted and a part of the community or the nation is as important as the feeling that he is a member of a family. He does not belong if he has a second-class citizenship. When he feels he does not belong, he is not eager to assume responsibilities of citizenship. Being unanchored, he is easy prey to divisive influences that are designed to tear a nation apart or to woo it to a foreign ideology.

"Franklin Roosevelt, like no other public figure in our history, was alive to this fact. And he knew how to fashion from it a positive and cohesive force in American life. He was in a very special sense the people's President because he made them feel that with him in the White House they shared the Presidency. The sense of sharing the Presidency gave even the most humble citizen a lively sense of belonging" (published in *Being an American* [New York: John Day Co., 1948], p. 88).

insistence upon mobility and our denial of status have been carried to excess. The fierceness of the mobility race generates tensions too severe for some people to bear, and fear of failure in this race generates a sense of insecurity which is highly injurious. Denial of status deprives the individual of one of his deepest psychological needs. Few societies have ever attempted to dispense with it, and most of them have acted to assure the individual of a certain niche in society, even if they were not prepared to offer a minimum wage or a more abundant life. Even where status appears to have been ejected, it sometimes comes in again by the back door: for instance, Americans who repudiated status in terms of an existing social order very often embraced mobility as leading to secure and desirable status in the social order of the future. In a country which possessed so little but could legitimately anticipate so much, it became genuine realism for the pioneer to identify himself with the prosperous future community which he was building rather than the squalid temporary settlement in which he lived. The imperceptible way in which the drive of mobility merges with the anticipation of status is suggested by the appeal used by a life insurance company which sells policies to provide for the future education of children and advertises with the picture of a small boy, over the caption, "He is going to college already."

It follows, then, that even where status has been publicly renounced, individuals continue to manifest, in a variety of ways, a deep psychological craving for the certitudes which it offers. The hazards and insecurities resulting from absence of status have sometimes caused an impulse, as Erich Fromm expresses it, to "escape from freedom." At times the appetite for the assurances which status gives has taken a pathological turn and contributed to the rise of the Fascist and Nazi and Communist dictatorships. Anyone who supposes that these phenomena were exclusively Italian or German or Russian has only to read *The Authoritarian Personality*, by T. W. Adorno and his associates (New York:

Harper & Bros., 1950), in order to see how corrosive an effect the frustrated craving for status has had upon personality in the United States.

In this connection, however, one should take the precaution of noting that the mobility drive and the doctrine of equality were not the only factors in the destruction of status, although they caused it to be repudiated morally. A fully articulated status system rested, technologically and socially, upon two bases which have now been very seriously impaired. One of these was the workman's satisfaction in and identification with his work. However humble his position, the craftsman knew that his community, with its economy of scarcity, needed his work, and, since it was his own work in the craft sense, he could regard his product as an extension of himself. The age of abundance, however, requiring a greater volume of processed goods, utilized machinery to meet the demand and made the former craftsman a more productive but less creative and less essential attendant upon the machine. The other basis was the position of the family as a matrix within which status was contained. Biologically and psychologically the family was a unit, and, so long as its members worked together, cultivating the crops, tending the animals, preparing the food and clothing, and practicing the handicrafts of early America, it was socially and economically a unit as well. The completeness of its integration assured to each member strong ties of relationship with the group. But again the age of abundance, arising from industrial growth and in turn stimulating further industrialization, caused a transformation. By compelling the individual to work outside the family, it divorced the family from the economy. For instance, it even took children, who had previously worked within the family, and made them work in the factory. The horror of child labor, as Drucker has observed, was not that it caused children to work (they had always worked) but that it deprived even those who most needed it of the protecting status found in the family relationship. By diffusing the focus which the family had given to social organization, the new economy made status a matter of several fragments—a man's status among his fellow-employees, his status in his neighborhood, his status at the bank—rather than one of a single, homogeneous social relationship. In this case the original whole was far greater than the sum of the subsequent parts.

The tenor of all these observations may seem, at first glance, utterly pessimistic. In summary, they seem to mean that the economic potentialities of our continent have caused us to subordinate other values to the realization of maximum wealth; that, in the process, we have committed ourselves to an impossible ideal—the ideal of mobility for everyone—with the consequence of causing tensions and insecurity for the individual; that we have made class distinctions more galling than ever by maintaining discriminations after the actual differences between classes have dwindled away; and that we have deprived men and women of the psychological values inherent in status. While abundance was producing these results through its emphasis on the mobility drive, it was at the same time striking at the foundations of status by substituting machine production for craft production and by bringing into operation an economy of which the family was not part. In short, everything would seem to lead to the conclusion that abundance has exacted a heavy psychological penalty for the physical gains which it has conferred.

In so far as there has been real damage, it would be fatuous to suppose that it can be to any great extent undone. No future policy is likely either to restore on a large scale the satisfactions of craftsmanship (which ought not to be idealized too much) or to give back to the family its function as a unifying focus for the multiple facets of life. Nor can we grasp either horn of the dilemma when bidden to choose between completely fulfilling the promise of equality, which is impossible, or abandoning it, which is unthinkable.

But, despite these factors, there is valid ground for hope that the same abundance which, in its developing stage, accentuated some of these conditions will, in its stage of fulfilment, ameliorate the same conditions.

What abundance did, in the period when its potentialities were being rapidly developed, was to throw out of balance the equilibrium between two forces, both of which are essential to a healthy society—the principle of mobility, which involves the welfare of man as an independent individual, and the principle of status, which involves his welfare as a member of the community. It destroyed this balance by making a good standard of living available for any man, while perpetuating a low standard as usual for most men. The continued low standard was the penalty for lack of mobility, and, as a consequence, mobility became mandatory. At the same time, the changes in the potential living standard began to make the system of status seem evil, for the status system had always consigned the vast majority to a life of bare sufficiency in an age when this was all that the existing economy would allow; but the growth of abundance, by making insufficiency unnecessary, made this aspect of status an avoidable one, thus making status itself seem needlessly harsh and unjust. In these circumstances, society exalted mobility inordinately, at the corresponding sacrifice of status.

Though these were the conditions, historically, under which abundance first began to make itself felt, it is important to recognize that they are not the conditions of abundance today. In our present economy, where there are fewer undeveloped opportunities demanding to be exploited, society does not need a population of mobile individuals as urgently as it did formerly. At the same time, the wide prevalence of a high standard of living means that the individual is no longer required to become mobile in order to share in the benefits which the economy has to offer. In proportion as this condition develops, mobility ought to become optional rather than obligatory. Where mobility was once the price of welfare, we now have a larger measure of welfare without mobility than any previous society in history, and this may enable us to relax the tensions of mobility, keeping it as an instrument for the self-fulfilment of the individual but dispensing with it as a social imperative.

In a comparable way, the fulfilment of abundance can free status of its one great historic blemish—its condemnation of the vast majority to a life of want. This opens the way for a more beneficent form of status which would emphasize the concepts of membership, of identity, of place in the community, and would minimize the hierarchical aspects, as, indeed, the new abundance has already minimized them by diminishing the physical differences in standards of dress, of diet, of housing, and of recreation among the various elements in society.

Admittedly, this restoration of the balance between mobility and status is still to be attained, and the consequences both of the excessive mobility drive and of lack of status are still conspicuous in our society. But there are some indications already that the emphases are beginning to change. Personnel offices in large business enterprises throughout the country are constantly at work to create a relationship which will give to employees a sense of membership and permanence in the organization; labor unions are concentrating their attention upon pensions, seniority, and the general question of tenure. In both cases, self-interest may be the motive, but, in so far as the efforts succeed, mobility will be diminished and status will be enhanced.

But, however these trends may work themselves out, it seems reasonably clear already that the present phase of abundance has begun to restore a balance by tending toward a permissive mobility, free of psychological tensions, and toward voluntary status, free of economic penalties. Thus there is every prospect that abundance will be a vital factor in controlling the status and mobility adjustments of the future, as it has been in determining the compulsion toward mobility and the repudiation of status which are such crucial factors in the American society of the present.

V. Democracy and Abundance

One of the most widely current phrases of the second World War was the designation of the countries in arms against the axis as the "freedom-loving nations." It was a conveniently vague term for masking the diversity of the cobelligerents, and its essential irony was not at the time apparent, even when it was applied to the Soviet Union. But, apart from its value as an expedient, the phrase undoubtedly gained great vitality from a genuine belief among Americans that the peoples of the world fall into two categories: those who love freedom and those who do not. Implicitly, we understood, of course, that we were the most devoted of all and that, while other countries might prove fickle in their affection, we could pride ourselves upon a record of constant fidelity. It was as if all the world had been presented with a choice between a right principle of government and a wrong one, and we, more than any others, had been unequivocal in choosing the right.

It is not unnatural, of course, for Americans to take this view of their political institutions. Americans have always been especially prone to regard all things as resulting from the free choice of a free will. Probably no people have so little determinism in their philosophy, and as individuals we have regarded our economic status, our matrimonial happiness, and even our eternal salvation as things of our own making. Why should we not then regard our political felicity, likewise, as a virtue which is also virtue's reward?

If this way of explaining ourselves to ourselves had no other result than to nourish our self-esteem, it would hardly be worthy of any special attention, for excessive national pride is in no sense peculiar to the United States. But our conception of democracy as a simple matter of moral choice has caused us to hope falsely that other countries will embrace democracy as we understand it, and to misconstrue badly the reasons for their failure to do so. It has even led us to condemn, quite unjustly, the countries which fail to establish a democracy like our own, as if it were plain obstinacy or even outright iniquity which explains their behavior.[1]

By viewing democracy simply as a question of political morality, we have blinded ourselves to the fact that, in every country, the system of government is a by-product of the general conditions of life, including, of course, the economic conditions, and that democracy, like any other system, is appropriate for countries where these conditions are suited to it and inappropriate for others with unsuitable conditions, or at least that it is vastly more appropriate for some than for others. Viewed in these terms, there is a strong case for believing that democracy is clearly most appropriate for countries which enjoy an economic surplus and least appropriate for countries where there is an economic insufficiency. In short, economic abundance is conducive to political democracy.[2]

At first glance this proposition may seem abjectly deterministic and may seem to imply that our democracy, like our climate, is a mere matter of luck, involving no merit. But it does not necessarily mean that we enjoy democracy without achieving it; rather, it means that we have achieved it less by sheer ideological devo-

1. "We have believed as a nation that other peoples had only to will our democratic institutions in order to repeat our own career" (Frederick Jackson Turner, *The Frontier in American History* [New York: Henry Holt & Co., 1920], p. 244).

2. "Political democracy came to the United States as the result of economic democracy. . . . This nation came to be marked by political institutions of a democratic type because it had, still earlier, come to be characterized in its economic life by democratic arrangements and practices" (J. Franklin Jameson, *The American Revolution Considered as a Social Movement* [Princeton: Princeton University Press, 1926], p. 41).

tion to the democratic principle than by the creation of economic conditions in which democracy will grow. In doing this, we have, of course, enjoyed the advantage of unequaled natural resources, but, as I have already sought to show, abundant physical endowments do not automatically or invariably produce an economic surplus for the area which possesses them. For instance, New England, poorly endowed by nature, became, in the nineteenth century, one of the richest regions of the United States, while the Cotton South, richly endowed, committed itself to a slave-labor system, a one-crop system, and an economy restricted to producing raw materials, which, in the end, left it the poorest part of the nation.

These instances and many others indicate that man may, through cultural processes, use environment well or use it ill; he may make his political system one of the instruments for such use; he may apply democratic devices for the purpose of developing or distributing abundance, and then he may use abundance as a base for the broadening and consolidation of his democracy. Or, to put it another way, he may use an economic surplus for the purpose of furthering a democratic system which will, in turn, enable him to increase further his economic surplus.

But, though this view does not, in a deterministic sense, deny man credit for democratic accomplishments, it does argue that he should distinguish very carefully the things for which credit is claimed. A nation may properly be proud that it has developed the economic means which enable it to afford a full-fledged democracy or that it has utilized democratic practices to create the economic base on which a democracy can be further broadened. But it cannot, with any validity, attribute its democracy to sheer moral and ideological virtue. Shaw stated the point forcibly in his Preface to *John Bull's Other Island,* when he said, "The virtues of the English soil are not less real because they consist of coal and iron, not of metaphysical sources of character. The virtues of Broadbent [the Englishman] are not less real because they are the virtues of the money that coal and iron have produced."

To understand why a democratic system depends upon an economic surplus, one has only to compare what a democracy offers to its citizens and what other regimes offer. All social systems, of course, seek to keep the bulk of their people contented, and all of them make promises of one kind or another in order to do this—some have promised a utopia in the indefinite future; others have offered, instead of real welfare, inexpensive distractions such as the bread and circuses of the Romans or the lotteries of modern Spain and Latin America; still others have attempted to provide real cradle-to-the-grave security. But however much or little a society, or a government acting for the society, may have to allot, it is axiomatic that it must not arouse expectations very much higher than it is able to satisfy. This means that it must not hold out the promise of opportunity unless there is a reasonable prospect of the opportunity's being fulfilled. It must not invite the individual to compete for prizes unless there are a substantial number of awards to be passed out.[3]

In all societies of economic insufficiency, which is the only kind that existed up to about two centuries ago, certain social conditions have been fixed and inevitable. The vast majority of the people were inescapably destined to heavy toil and bare subsistence, and the economic surplus in excess of such bare subsistence was not sufficient to give leisure and abundance to more than a tiny minority. In these circumstances, certainly the society could not afford either the economic or the emotional costs of conducting a great social steeplechase for the purpose of selecting a handful of winners to occupy the few enviable posi-

3. For extended, systematic consideration of the manner in which a society motivates its members to perform the roles necessary to the functioning of the social system see Talcott Parsons, *Essays in Sociological Theory* (Glencoe, Ill.: Free Press, 1949), and Robert K. Merton, *Social Theory and Social Structure* (Glencoe, Ill.: Free Press, 1949).

tions.[4] It was much sounder public policy to assign these positions by an arbitrary system of status and at the same time to assign to the great bulk of the people the burdens which most of them were destined to bear regardless of what regime was in power. Under a system of subordination transmitted by heredity, social competition, with its attendant loss of energy through friction, was avoided; the status-bound individual often gained a sense of contentment with his lot and even of dignity within his narrow sphere, and all that he sacrificed for this psychological advantage was a statistically negligible chance for advancement. Moreover, in a relatively static and relatively simple society such as that of Tudor or Stuart England, the problems of government were not very intricate, and the only qualities required in the local ruling class were integrity and a willingness to accept responsibility. These qualities could usually be found and could readily be transmitted even in a squirearchy of low intellectual attainments, and therefore there was no need to recruit widely for leadership, as a society must do when it requires intelligence, specialized skill, and adaptability in its administration.

A country with inadequate wealth, therefore, could not safely promise its citizens more than security of status—at a low level in the social hierarchy and with a meager living. But this promise is, in its denial of equality, by definition, undemocratic. A democracy, by contrast, setting equality as its goal, must promise opportunity, for the goal of equality becomes a mockery unless there is some means of attaining it. But in promising opportunity, the democracy is constantly arousing expectations which it lacks the current means to fulfil and is betting on its ability to procure the necessary means by the very act of stimulating people to demand them and go after them. It is constantly educating large

4. "And yet, Burke might have countered, once the masses were fated by the laws of political economy to toil in misery, what else was the idea of equality but a cruel bait to goad mankind into self-destruction" (Karl Polanyi, *The Great Transformation* [New York: Rinehart & Co., 1944], p. 119).

numbers of people without waiting to see whether jobs requiring education are available for all of them; it does this in the expectation that the supply will create a demand and that a society constantly rising in the level of its education will constantly generate new posts in which educated people are needed. Also, democracy is forever encouraging individuals to determine their own goals and set their own courses toward these goals, even though only a small proportion can attain complete success; the time and effort of many may be wasted in the pursuit, but the advantage to society of having the maximum number of people developing their maximum potentialities of intellect and personality is thought to justify the social cost.

All this is very well and works admirably if the country following these practices has the necessary physical resources and human resourcefulness to raise the standard of living, to create new occupational opportunities, and to find outlets for the abilities of an ever increasing class of trained men. But it must have this endowment to begin with, or it is certain to suffer intensely from the social waste that results from giving training which cannot be utilized and from the psychological damage that results when a competition has an excess of participants and a paucity of rewards. In short, to succeed as a democracy, a country must enjoy an economic surplus to begin with or must contrive to attain one.[5]

If this is true, it means that the principles of democracy are not universal truths, ignored during centuries of intellectual darkness and brought to light at last in the age of the American Revolution, but rather that democracy is the foremost by far of the many advantages which our economic affluence has bought

5. John Taylor of Caroline said, "Wealth, like suffrage, must be considerably distributed to sustain a democratick republic; and hence, whatever draws a considerable proportion of either into a few hands will destroy it" (*An Inquiry into the Principles and Policy of the Government of the United States* [Fredericksburg, Va., 1814], pp. 274–75).

for us. To say this, of course, is also to say that, when we propose world-wide adoption of democracy, our problem is not merely to inspire a belief in it but to encourage conditions conducive to it. About a year ago an English visitor in America made a comparison between socialism and free-enterprise democracy, which illustrated extremely well, though quite unwittingly, the reliance of democracy upon these conditions.

The comparison was based on a contrast between the ways in which the two systems in question might deal with the departure of a passenger train. Under a thoroughgoing system of socialism, said the description, the seating of all passengers would be directed. Station attendants would supervise the seating of every ticket-holder. They would arbitrarily place together people who did not want to sit together or place individuals in seats with ventilation or sunlight which those individuals particularly disliked. At the scheduled hour of departure, they would delay the train in order to complete their arrangements. Cost of operations would be increased, passengers vexed, and timetables disrupted.

In a democracy of the American kind, said the comparison, those who particularly want good seats come early, while those who do not care come late, quite prepared to accept what is left. Individuals indulge their own preferences and aversions as to sunlight and in the choice of neighbors. They distribute themselves, automatically and to the maximum satisfaction of all concerned, throughout the train, and all this is accomplished without supervision, without expense, and without delay.

Like all analogies, this one probably has its pitfalls; but, without stopping to look for them, can we not observe one major unstated assumption in the description of the democratic train? It is the simple assumption that *there will be enough seats for everyone;* that the average passenger stands a reasonably good chance of finding one that will satisfy him. If the passenger train symbolizes the American economy, this assumption is valid, but for other countries it may or may not be valid, and certainly it is the sufficiency of seats, quite as much as the method of seat-selection, which makes the democratic system work.

Not only has the presence of more than enough seats, more than enough rewards for those who strive, made the maintenance of a democratic system possible in America; it has also given a characteristic tone to American equalitarianism as distinguished from the equalitarianism of the Old World. Essentially, the difference is that Europe has always conceived of redistribution of wealth as necessitating the expropriation of some and the corresponding aggrandizement of others; but America has conceived of it primarily in terms of giving to some without taking from others. Hence, Europe cannot think of altering the relationship between the various levels of society without assuming a class struggle; but America has altered and can alter these relationships without necessarily treating one class as the victim or even, in an ultimate sense, the antagonist of another. The European mind often assumes implicitly that the volume of wealth is fixed; that most of the potential wealth has already been converted into actual wealth; that this actual wealth is already in the hands of owners; and, therefore, that the only way for one person or group to secure more is to wrest it from some other person or group, leaving that person or group with less. The British Labour party, for instance, has, I believe, placed greater emphasis upon the heavy taxation of the wealthy and less upon the increase of productive capacity than an American labor party might have done. The American mind, by contrast, often assumes implicitly that the volume of wealth is dynamic, that much potential wealth still remains to be converted; and that diverse groups—for instance, capital and labor—can take more wealth out of the environment by working together than they can take out of one another by class warfare.

European radical thought is prone to demand that the man of property be stripped of his carriage and his fine clothes; but

American radical thought is likely to insist, instead, that the ordinary man is entitled to mass-produced copies, indistinguishable from the originals. Few Americans feel entirely at ease with the slogan "Soak the rich," but the phrase "Deal me in" springs spontaneously and joyously to American lips.

This American confidence that our abundance will suffice for the attainment of all the goals of social justice is evident throughout the greater part of our national history. Even before the American Revolution, squatters who had entered into illegal occupation of land on the Pennsylvania frontier justified their action by declaring that "it was against the law of God and nature that so much land should be idle while so many Christians wanted it to labor on to raise bread." They did not contend, it is worth noticing, that it was wrong in general for man to want for bread. They probably had been taught to regard want as part of the order of nature; but, where so much land was available, then it was wrong for men to want. In other words, the availability of an economic surplus altered the standards of social justice.

It has been altering them ever since. It enabled Dr. Townsend to win a vast following for the belief that it was wrong for old people to receive less than thirty dollars every Thursday; it enabled Upton Sinclair to come within an ace of being elected governor of what is now the second state in the Union, on a platform that demanded an end of poverty in California. It was this same attitude of mind on which Huey P. Long capitalized in his "share-our-wealth" program—and capitalized to such good effect that he became for a while Franklin Roosevelt's most dangerous adversary. In his formal argument, Long employed a simple fallacy: he computed the value of America's wealth, developed and undeveloped, liquid and nonliquid, and then proceeded to treat the total sum as if it were in the form of cash available for distribution. Granted the validity of his calculation, the phrase "every man a king" did not seem excessive. But, despite this sophistry, Long was not relying primarily upon the arithmetical naïveté of the American people; he was relying upon their belief in the inexhaustible plenty of North America and in their own unrestrained right to enjoy this plenty without brain trust or dogma.

Long, Townsend, and Sinclair have provided striking though extreme examples of the American faith in plenty; but it is perhaps more revealing to consider a program which gained the support of a clear majority of all Americans—namely, the New Deal. For Franklin Roosevelt, too, was an apostle of abundance and, accordingly, of the view that the one-third who were unfortunate could be cared for without detriment to existing interests. Although hated in conservative circles as an expropriator and a fomenter of class antagonisms, Roosevelt in fact attempted to create a real balance between various class interests, such as those of labor and those of management; and this balance was predicated on an idea which was the very antithesis of the class struggle—the idea that no one need lose anything: debts were not scaled down, mortgages were not canceled, imminent bankruptcies which would have paved the way for nationalization were not permitted to occur. Even "the unscrupulous moneychangers," as Roosevelt called them, were not driven from the temples of finance. They were simply required to suspend operations for a brief time. Landlords collected farm benefits; industrialists under the NRA secured indulgence for monopolistic practices that had been under fire from more conservative administrations for forty years; while little businesses were protected by Thurman Arnold and the TNEC. At the nadir of the Depression, when capitalism was fearfully vulnerable and almost unresisting to attack and when many doctrinaires would have said that the overthrow of capitalism was the prerequisite to reform, Roosevelt unhesitatingly assumed that the country could afford to pay capitalism's ransom and to buy reform, too. One of his most irritating and most successful qualities was his habit of assuming that benefits could be granted without costs being felt—an assumption rooted in his faith in the potentialities of the American economy.

Going beyond Roosevelt himself, it is interesting to consider the attitude of the American people as a whole toward the idea of class struggle. Antipathy to the concept is a well-known American trait, and it is frequently associated with or attributed to America's faith in the ideal of equality and America's reluctance to admit that social stratification exists. Certainly this commitment to the ideal of equality has a deep bearing; but is not our hostility to the class-struggle concept also linked with our reluctance to entertain the thought that American wealth has ceased to grow, that we can no longer raise the standard of living at one point without lowering it somewhere else?

Occasionally, one encounters the statement that Americans believe in leveling up rather than in leveling down. The truth of the assertion is more or less self-evident, but the basic meaning is less so. Clearly, if one is leveling a fixed number of items, say, personal incomes, the very process of leveling implies the reduction of the higher ones. But in order to raise the lower without reducing the higher, to level *up*, it is necessary to increase the total of all the incomes—that is, to introduce new factors instead of solving the problem with the factors originally given. And it is by this stratagem of refusing to accept the factors given, of drawing on nature's surplus and on technology's tricks, that America has often dealt with her problems of social reform.

This, in turn, may explain another distinctive feature of the American record, and that is the relative lack of intellectualism in its reform or radical movements. For instance, by European standards the Populists of the late nineteenth century, and even more the Progressives of the early twentieth, would have seemed incredibly muddled, sentimental, and superficial in their thinking. European radicalism almost invariably has had a highly articulated rationale, a fully developed doctrinal system. European radicals have kept their ideological weapons sharpened to razor edge, so that they are ever ready to follow logic through the most complex maze or to split the hairs of heresy in disputes over minor points of doctrine. They do this, in part, I believe, because the social problems with which they deal are relatively fixed, and disciplined intelligence is the one means through which they can hope to attain a solution. But the social problems of America were not at all fixed, and their mutability has made logical solutions unnecessary.

Our practice, indeed, has been to overleap problems—to by-pass them—rather than to solve them. For instance, in the 1880's and 1890's there seemed to be three major public problems—the problem of a shrinking bullion supply; the problem of the control of an entire industry by a small group of monopolists, like John D. Rockefeller and his associates in the oil industry; and the problem of regulation of the railroads, which enjoyed a natural monopoly of transportation. Reformers struggled with all three of these problems, and various political solutions were proposed: the adoption of a bimetallic currency to relieve the bullion stringency, the enactment of an anti-trust law to curb Mr. Rockefeller, and the adoption of an Interstate Commerce Act to protect the shipper vis-à-vis the railroads. But in each case technological change interposed to relieve the acuteness of the problem or even to make it obsolete: the discovery of new gold supplies in the Klondike and of new methods of recovering gold reversed the process of shrinkage in the bullion supply; the discovery of the vast new deposits of oil in Texas and elsewhere undermined the dominance of Rockefeller in the oil industry as no legislative prohibition was ever able to do; and the introduction of trucks moving over a network of national highways ended the natural monopoly of transportation by the railroads before Congress ceased the long quest for a legislative solution.

There is a widespread belief in the United States that the basic policy of our government underwent a sudden change about twenty years ago, with the advent of the New Deal. According to this belief, the American Republic had been a thoroughgoing laissez faire state during its first century and a half—a state where government scrupulously refrained from intervention in the economic sphere, and private enterprise alone shaped the country's economic progress. Then, it is supposed, an abrupt reversal of policy took place, and, turning our backs upon the principles that had guided us to our earlier economic triumphs, we embraced a paternalistic program of governmental regulation and control which started us on the road to the welfare state. This view is probably most widely prevalent in conservative circles, but among people who are left of center there is also a widespread belief that government in the nineteenth and early twentieth centuries held aloof from economic problems and that this negative attitude continued until the time of Franklin Roosevelt, who followed a trail blazed by the Progressives and asserted a more constructive function for public authority. In short, left and right are in dispute as to the merit of this change, but they are inclined to agree that a complete change took place.

Without denying that a major transformation occurred, we need to be aware of the strands of continuity, as well as of the shifts and new departures in our history. If we are to appreciate the links with the past, we must recognize that laissez faire was not the unique principle of policy in our eighteenth- and nineteenth-century development but that one of the key principles was certainly the constant endeavor of government to make the economic abundance of the nation accessible to the public. The tactics by which this was done changed as the form of abundance itself changed, but the basic purpose—to keep our population in contact with the sources of wealth—has remained steadily in the ascendant throughout our history.

In the early nineteenth century the major form in which abundance presented itself was the fertility of unsettled land. For a people of whom 90 per cent followed agricultural pursuits, access to abundance meant opportunity to settle the new lands. The government responded by a series of land laws, beginning with the Ordinance of 1785 and extending far past the Homestead Act of 1862, which made land progressively easier for settlers to attain, until at last they could acquire title to 160 acres absolutely free. Over the years, while this was happening, some eminently public spirited men like John Quincy Adams contended for a program that would have conserved the assets of the public domain by distributing it gradually and on a basis that would yield revenue to the Treasury; but all such proposals were defeated, and quick settlement was stimulated even by legislation which encouraged squatters to occupy the land before it had been opened to public entry. Widespread access to wealth was preferred over the public capitalization of a great economic asset.

Relatively early, however, it became clear that access to soil did not mean access to wealth unless it was accompanied by access to market. Fertile soil remained a mere potentiality when its products could not reach the consumer. The market was the source of wealth to which access was needed, and again government responded by providing the internal improvements which would give such access. Sometimes the federal government did this, as, for instance, by the construction of the Cumberland Pike; sometimes the state governments took the initiative, as New York did with the digging of the Erie Canal; and sometimes government did not execute the project itself but encouraged private interests to do so by offering such tangible inducements as direct financial support, use of the public credit, and use of the power of eminent domain. Even in so great a project as the building of the first transcontinental railroad, the government virtually furnished all the funds, and, though the ownership was private, a congressman from New York could truthfully point out that the government in fact had built the railroads.

Later still, the wealth to which access was needed appeared

increasingly in forms that could not be handled by the individual acting as a solitary operator. Iron resources, coal resources, petroleum resources, water-power resources, and other physical assets promised to raise the standard of living; but the only means of access to their value was through large-scale concentration of capital and labor. Again, government responded by facilitating the means of access: it made easy the process of concentration by sanctioning the wide use of the practice of incorporation; it assured the new corporations, through judicial interpretation of the Fourteenth Amendment, that they would enjoy the fullest legal security and even advantage; by the tariffs of the Civil War and post–Civil War periods, it guaranteed the corporations control of the American market. In return they did what was expected of them: they converted potential wealth into usable wealth, wastefully, selfishly, and ruthlessly in many cases, but quickly—and results were the primary thing demanded of them.

By the third decade of the twentieth century, the form in which wealth appeared had again altered drastically. No longer did it consist in natural resources of soil or subsoil, requiring to be put into operation. Access to wealth was now dependent upon the continued movement of the production lines rather than upon the throwing open of untapped resources. In these circumstances, the operation of the business cycle, manifesting itself in the great Depression, seemed to block access to wealth as completely as the barriers of physical distance had blocked it a century earlier. In both cases, though the overt circumstances seemed wholly dissimilar, Americans found consolation in the same basic and comforting conviction—that abundance was there, and the problem was not to create it or to get along without it but simply to find how to get at it. And in both cases government responded with steps to provide access. If access depended upon the creation of purchasing power, government under the New Deal was ready to create it by spending, lending, priming the pump, and enacting minimum-wage laws; if it depended upon the capacity of workers to bargain collectively, government was ready to confer that capacity by law; if it depended upon securing industry against some of the hazards of competition, government offered a National Industrial Recovery Act to remove these hazards.

Writers on public questions often assume that in our early history we had a basic commitment to individualism and that we have recently abandoned this traditional principle just for the sake of security. But what we really were committed to was realizing on the potentialities of our unmatched assets and raising our standard of living. Because the standard of living involves comfort and material things, a basic concern with it is commonly regarded as ignoble; yet, as I have already suggested, it is only because we have attained a relatively high standard of living that we can afford to own and operate a democratic system. But, whether noble or not, our commitment to abundance was primary, and individualism was sanctioned as the very best means of fulfilling the possibilities of abundance. When it ceased to be the best means, we modified it with a readiness alarming to people who had supposed that it was the individualism itself which was basic. We did this because a great many people had never regarded it, at bottom, as more than a means to an end. The politics of our democracy was a politics of abundance rather than a politics of individualism,[6] a politics of increasing our wealth quickly rather than of dividing it precisely, a politics which smiled both on those who valued abundance as a means to safeguard freedom and on those who valued freedom as an aid in securing abundance.

In so far as Americans have succeeded in equating abundance and freedom, it becomes something of an abstraction to question

6. "Thomas Carlyle once said to an American: 'Ye may boast o' yer dimocracy, or any ither 'cracy, or any kind o' poleetical roobish; but the reason why yer laboring folk are so happy is thoth ye have a vost deal o' land for a verra few people'" (Josiah Strong, *Our Country* [1885], p. 153).

which is the means and which is the end. The historical analyst may itch to discover which one is basic and which derivative, but the purpose of Americans, generally, will be to make the two coincide in such a way that, as factors, they cannot be isolated. In this sense it may seem somewhat metaphysical to make heavy-handed distinctions between these two ingredients—freedom and abundance—which are to such a great extent fused in American democratic thought.

But, though Americans have caused freedom and abundance to converge, the two are not by nature prone to convergence, and for the world at large they have not been closely linked. Consequently, when America, out of her abundance, preaches the gospel of democracy to countries which see no means of attaining abundance, the message does not carry the meaning which it is meant to convey. No other part of American activity has been so consistently and so completely a failure as our attempt to export democracy. At this point, the duality between abundance and freedom in the American democratic formula ceases to be abstract and becomes painfully concrete, for it is the lack of understanding of what we have to offer to the rest of the world that has vitiated our efforts to fulfil a national mission which we undertook with real dedication and for which we have made real sacrifices. But the discussion of this aspect of the relation between democracy and abundance will involve a consideration of the world relations of the American Republic, and this is so extensive a subject that it must be left for another chapter.

VI. Abundance and the Mission of America

From the very inception of the American Republic, the United States has constantly supposed that it had a message for the world, even a mission to perform in the world.[1] That message, we were convinced, was democracy; that mission, the exemplification to all the world of the merit of democratic institutions— even the propagation of such institutions. From the outset, our Declaration of Independence concerned itself not simply with the rights of the colonists or the equality of British subjects but with the equality of all men and their universal right to liberty. This sense of national mission was once reflected with special clarity in a eulogy which Abraham Lincoln pronounced on Henry Clay: "Mr. Clay," he declared, "loved his country partly because it was his own country, but mostly because it was a free country . . . he burned with a zeal for its advancement . . . because he saw in such the advancement . . . and glory of human liberty, human right, and human nature."[2]

Also, from the beginning, the American people have experienced a long succession of disappointments in which prospects for the realization of the American mission appeared to present themselves but were never fulfilled. Our government under the Constitution had not been in operation for more than six weeks when the first hopeful signs appeared that our ideals were about to spread. The Estates-General met outside Paris, and Thomas

1. Ralph H. Gabriel, in *The Course of American Democratic Thought since 1815* (New York: Ronald Press Co., 1940), regards the idea of the mission of America as one of the three basic themes in our democratic philosophy.

2. Speech at Springfield, July 6, 1852, printed in Roy P. Basler (ed.), *Collected Works of Abraham Lincoln* (New Brunswick, N.J.: Rutgers University Press, 1953), II, 126.

Jefferson, who was on the scene, rejoiced at the prospect of a French application of American libertarian principles. In the following July, when French opponents of reaction stormed the Bastille, that ancient landmark of despotism and oppression, the Marquis de Lafayette, who was now rapidly becoming a "hero of two worlds," sent the key of the prison to George Washington. Here, seemingly, was the almost perfect symbol of the fact that the American mission was already, with extraordinary promptness, beginning to succeed.

But after that the revolution entered the phase of the guillotine and the Terror, and America was, for the first time, brought reluctantly to the recognition of what she has been forced to recognize so often since, namely, that American ideals were not working out according to American expectations. American liberals were, for the first time, put on a spot where they have repeatedly found themselves in the last hundred and sixty years —that is, they were compelled to overlook much of the bloodshed, the violence, the exercise of despotic authority in the name of the people and were obliged to make the most of the basic similarity between American revolutionary and French revolutionary principles. After the lapse of a few more years, Napoleon emerged as the supreme power in the land of liberty, equality, and fraternity, and by that time even the most ardent American Jacobin could no longer keep up the pretense that France was merely applying American beliefs in her own distinctively Gallic way.

After a hundred and sixty years, this cycle by which revolts against despotism mature into despotisms under new management has become a painfully familiar story, but it required more than this first disillusionment of the Jeffersonian Francophiles to disillusion the American people. Indeed, faith in America's democratic mission was far too robust to yield to a single disconcerting experience, and we continued to hail the gleam of liberty wherever it showed itself. When Greece revolted, Byron and Shelley were not without their American counterparts in enthusiasm for the Greek cause. The students of Yale College, to take but one example, collected a fund of $500 to be sent to those in revolt. When the Latin-American colonies of Spain rose up against the Bourbons, Henry Clay hailed their heroic action as if it were Lexington and Concord all over again, and Congress was ready to extend recognition at once. The administration refused to move until it had completed negotiations with Spain for the purchase of Florida and for the settlement of the claims of the two countries in Oregon and in Texas. But then President Monroe accorded recognition immediately, and what is much more important, served notice in his famous message to Congress in December, 1823, that the United States would oppose any European interference with these states and that we regarded the political system of the New World as being essentially different from that of the Old.

Here again we find the hope, so often reaffirmed, that Latin-American democracy would turn out to be North American democracy adapted to the tropics and to the Southern Hemisphere. A few men with insight, like John Quincy Adams, knew it would not, and everyone else has now learned that revolts against despotism south of the border frequently end at the same destination as revolts against despotism in other parts of the world.

In some respects, the only revolutions with which the American people could feel completely satisfied were the ones that did not succeed. After every revolution that failed, we were free to assume that its success would have fulfilled our ideals and were free to extend our hospitality to the revolutionists who were no longer welcome at home. Sometimes this welcome took spectacular forms, as when Congress received Louis Kossuth, or when Lincoln sent Carl Schurz, one of the revolutionists and later *émigrés* of 1848, back to the Old World as minister of the United States to the court of Madrid, or when Eamon de Valera and other Irish patriots enjoyed triumphal tours in this country. At other times the welcome was less conspicuous, but we may be sure that Garibaldi's hatred of Hapsburg rule in Italy and Leon Trotsky's animosity toward the Romanovs did not make the Italian visitor any less acceptable when he lived on Staten Island or the Russian revolutionary any less at home when he lived on the lower East Side of New York.

We continued to hope that American liberty could go abroad and still remain liberty as we knew her, and, in fact, we never faltered in seeking to promote this end. The spectacle of Cuba struggling to be free provided popular support for the Spanish-American War, though it ended in a Platt Amendment for Cuba and an occupation for the Philippine Islands because we could not bear to face what these two aspirants to liberty were likely to do with their freedom. The establishment of a republic in China in 1912 was hailed with a sentimental enthusiasm that prevented us then, or later, from scrutinizing Chinese conditions in a realistic way.

Later still, when we engaged in two major world wars, we could not bring ourselves to confront and accept the sacrifices that would be required, without some conviction that our historic mission would now be fostered on a global scale. Technically, the first World War may have had as its *casus belli* for the United States the question of the violation by submarines of neutral rights, but the dynamic of the war for Americans was not to vindicate the rights of visit and search; it was "to make the world safe for democracy." Perhaps it is true that many Americans recognized a certain spacious quality in this formula and that they backed away from it in 1919, but there is little doubt that Americans regarded the force which they called "Kaiserism" as a menace to democracy on the world scene and felt, in terms of our mission, an obligation to liquidate it and thus to leave an open field for democratic advance.

When we were, for the second time, confronted with world

war in 1939, Franklin Roosevelt avoided the highly idealistic, highly altruistic formulas which Wilson had invoked, and, indeed, he made a special effort to be "realistic" and to emphasize America's immediate stake in the result. But he, too, felt the need for the moral dynamism gained by asserting universal rights for man: hence the Atlantic Charter and the four freedoms, which seemed so much more human and therefore more universal in their appeal than Wilson's "points," whose multiplicity had led Clemenceau to observe that "le bon Dieu" had only ten but President Wilson required fourteen.

Today, when the four freedoms seem as much an illusion as the Big Four who were jointly to underwrite them, the frustration of the belief in an American mission is too poignant to admit of dispassionate comment. Consistently, throughout our history, we have assumed that we had a message for the world, a democratic message, and, some would say, a message of redemption. Consistently we have scanned the horizon, looking for signs that the message was being received. Hopefully we have attempted to convince ourselves that other movements were intrinsically at one with our own, despite local differences of complexion: that French Jacobinism was American democracy reacting against a greater accumulation of grievances and acts of oppression than America had known; that Latin-American *caudillos* were merely American political bosses strutting in gaudy uniforms; that the Soviets of 1919 and 1920 were merely extending American political democracy into the economic orbit and were carrying on from where we had stopped; that the Chinese Communists were, at bottom, Jeffersonian democrats who mouthed the phrases of Marx but thought the thoughts of the independent agrarian man.

Ironically, those who have embraced the principles of democracy—those who have adopted the system that we desired to spread—have been indebted to us only in a minor sense for their ideas. Britain enacted her Reform Bill of 1832 at a time when

America was regarded with widespread contempt by the British; Canada received her dominion status upon the recommendation of a British peer and without any instigation by the United States; Australia and New Zealand worked out their democratic regimes almost as if the United States were on another planet; and the republics of western Europe owe their self-government very much more to European socialist thought than to American democratic thought.

Although democracy in the American style never seemed to gain ascendancy in other parts of the globe, there was a long interval, extending over most of the nineteenth century, during which American ideals seemed a beacon light to poor and humble folk all over the world. Millions of these poor came to America because it was a refuge for the oppressed, and millions of others who remained at home were inspired by the American dream. The moral authority of our ideals of equality, of freedom, and of opportunity was immense, and we were entitled to believe that for every aristocrat who disparaged us or condescended to us there were scores of plain men and women who shared in and were heartened by our aspirations for human welfare. The rapidity and eagerness with which our immigrants embraced Americanism gave tangible proof of this response, and thus our people, who have always been solicitous for the approval of others, could find comfort in the assurance that the heart of humanity responded to the creed of our democracy. This assurance went far to mitigate our disappointment at the failure of American democracy to take root overseas.

But today this consolation has utterly vanished, and we now harbor few illusions as to the affection which we can command from the mass of humanity. Ever since the days of Calvin Coolidge, when Uncle Sam first heard himself being called "Uncle Shylock," we have grown increasingly used to finding American motives misrepresented and American ideals greeted with skepticism and indifference. In the last decade many Americans have come sadly to believe that the only influence which we can command is of that precarious kind which is bought and paid for, not once but repeatedly. In so far as we do find friends, they are less among the oppressed than among the propertied and conservative classes.

In these circumstances one is almost constrained to wonder whether, in reality, we have had a message for the world at all. If we did, why this series of frustrations in delivering it? Why have 'we, who applauded at the birth of so many revolutions, so consistently found those revolutions defeating the very ends which we hoped they would promote? Why has our country, which championed the cause of ordinary humanity, received its most vicious attacks from the spokesmen of the proletariat?

In some respects this is the question behind all the questions which confront America today, and, as such, it has an over-whelming importance which should discourage a casual approach. The immense difficulty of the problem automatically discredits all simple solutions, and it is challenge enough even to define the problem. It is, therefore, with some hesitation that I point out one possible aspect in which the factor of American abundance bears upon this problem and thus may be of some use in defining it, even though it could hardly be of any direct use in dealing with it.

The thought is not original with me, but what I would suggest is this: that we have been historically correct in supposing that we had a revolutionary message to offer but we have been mistaken in our concept of what that message was. We supposed that our revelation was "democracy revolutionizing the world," but in reality it was "abundance revolutionizing the world"—a message which we did not preach and scarcely understood ourselves, but one which was peculiarly able to preach its own gospel without words.

It is perhaps significant that it took a European to perceive the true impact which the United States had upon the rest of the world. As early as 1932, André Siegfried, in an address to a group of French Protestant businessmen, made these very pregnant observations: "The West," he said, "has thought for a long time, not without a certain naïveté, that it represented spirituality in the world. But is spirituality really the message we have taken along with us everywhere? What has been borrowed from us, as I have so often observed, is our mechanisms. Today, in the most remote, most ancient villages, one finds the automobile, the cinema, the radio, the telephone, the phonograph, not to mention the airplane, and it is not the white men, nor the most civilized, who display the greatest enthusiasm for them."[3]

This comment applies to the influence of Western civilization as a whole, but, with specific reference to America, Siegfried said, "The United States is presiding at a general reorganization of the ways of living throughout the entire world."

As to what we have imparted, "the one really new gospel we have introduced is the revelation, after centuries of passively endured privations, that a man may at last free himself of poverty, and, most fantastic innovation of all, that he may actually enjoy his existence. . . . And so, without our wishing it, or even knowing it, we appear as the terrible instigators of social change and revolution."

If Siegfried is correct, we were right in supposing that we wielded a revolutionary force but were wrong in supposing it to be an ideological one, when it was, in fact, material. It was not our ideal of democracy but our export of goods and gadgets, of cheap, machine-produced grain and magic-working medicines, which opened new vistas to the human mind and thus made us "the terrible instigators of social change and revolution." Isabel Cary Lundberg, who wrote about this revolutionary dynamic in *Harper's Magazine*[4] and who there quoted Siegfried's sugges-

3. Quoted in Isabel Cary Lundberg, "World Revolution, American Plan," *Harper's Magazine*, CXCVII (December, 1948), 38–46.
    4. *Ibid.*

tions, has observed that every American who was overseas between 1941 and 1945 was in some respects a revolutionary agent of social change. What was it, she asks, that "the native populations everywhere wanted of the G.I., the Air Force pilot, the gob, and the Seabee? They wanted what the vast majority of the world's population, European and non-European wants: the wrist watch, fountain pen, cigarettes, flashlight, chocolate bars, chewing gum, cameras, pocket knives, pills to kill pain, vaccines to save lives, hospital beds with clean sheets, hand soap and shaving soap, gadgets and gewgaws of every description, the jeep, the truck, and *white bread*. Very few Americans, picking and choosing among the piles of white bread in a super-market, have ever appreciated the social standing of white bread elsewhere in the world. To be able to afford white bread is a dream that awaits fulfillment for billions of the world's population. To afford it signifies that one enjoys all the comforts of life."

At this point it is well to enter a qualifier and to recognize specifically that the United States did not invent either white bread or the sulfa drugs or, at large, the concept of an improved standard of living. The industrial countries of western Europe practiced imperialism not only to assure themselves of supplies of raw materials but also to provide an outlet for their industrial production, and it was western Europe as much as the United States which introduced the wonders of industry to the rest of the world. Nevertheless, the United States has certainly played a far greater part than any other country in displaying to the world the variety and magic of the new abundance, and it has also done more than any other to disseminate the belief that this abundance may actually be placed within the grasp of ordinary men and women. The films that come out of Hollywood, for instance, have presented conspicuous consumption not as a mere practice but, one might say, as a system and an act of faith.

For a country destined, as ours has been, to play such a role it was a tragic fallacy that we conceived of democracy as an absolute value, largely ideological in content and equally valid in any environment, instead of recognizing that our own democratic system is one of the major by-products of our abundance, workable primarily because of the measure of our abundance. In the preceding chapter, I have already attempted to discuss this point in a context of domestic affairs and to show our error in thinking of democracy as a system which we have because, out of our superior political wisdom and virtue, we chose it, when, in fact, any credit that we give to ourselves ought to be for creating the conditions that would enable it to work and would enable us to afford it. On the domestic scene, the fallacy was more or less academic in its consequences, which is perhaps why we have been slow to perceive it. The only adverse result was to bring us to the right operative conclusions for the wrong reasons.

But on the international front this fallacy has had most far-reaching results, in that it has consistently impelled us to proselyte for converts to the democratic faith in places where the economic prerequisites for democracy have not been established. This, I believe, has a great deal to do with the widespread impression in the world that the Americans are, somehow, hypocrites. In our own country the promise of equality meant the right to advance, without discrimination, to easily attainable ends. Hence the principle of equality could be upheld with genuine sincerity. Freedom meant the removal of barriers to advancement from one position to another, more advantageous one. But in countries where even decency, much less comfort, lay beyond the point of attainability for most people—where the number of advantageous positions was negligible—it seemed a kind of deception to offer the individual as good a chance as anyone to compete for nonexistent prizes or to assure him of his freedom to go where he wished, when there was, in fact, nowhere to go.

This anomalous relationship between the permissive and the protective aspects of freedom has always required adjustment, both at the domestic and at the international level. Thus Franklin

Roosevelt, who, on the domestic front, shifted the emphasis from freedom as immunity to control, to freedom as immunity to social privation, also recognized the need for giving new connotations to the term "freedom" on the international scene. Hence his four freedoms—freedom of speech, freedom of religion, freedom from want, and freedom from fear—were two parts freedom in the classic liberal sense and two parts security under the label of "freedom."

If Roosevelt had been able to fulfil his formula, the whole nature of this problem would be different; but he was not, and we revert to the fact that American liberals throughout our history have misunderstood the nature of our own economic revolution and have also misunderstood what the revolutionists of other countries wanted. Jefferson and his landowning, independent, backwoods farmers, who had conducted a political revolution against Britain without social upheaval, were not prepared for the convulsions that an oppressed class of serfs and a Paris mob would regard as a necessary part of any reform that was worth making in France. Henry Clay and the expansive westerners did not appreciate that in Latin America, behind the few idealists who believed in liberty, there was a local ruling class which saw no reason why absentees in Europe should continue to share in the exploitation of the Indians and who proposed to monopolize this exploitation for themselves. The idealists who felt it a national obligation to liberate Cuba in 1898 did not appreciate that the Cubans were revolting against economic conditions which resulted even more from the McKinley Tariff than from the iniquities of Bourbon misrule. American liberals in 1919 and 1920 failed to grasp the fact that Russian revolutionaries were overthrowing the ruthless regime of the tsars not because they wanted to substitute a more humanitarian regime in its place but because they wanted to substitute a more efficient ruthlessness, and one which would be operated by a different class.

The most effective means by which we could have promoted

humanitarian and democratic principles abroad was not by applauding revolutions conducted in the name of such principles but by imparting to other parts of the world the means that we have developed for raising the standard of living. On the face of it, this assertion may seem inconsistent with the whole thesis of these chapters, namely, that the United States enjoyed a richer endowment than other countries and that this physical heritage has influenced our past history and our present society in distinctive ways. But no less important than the original, easily accessible wealth was the fact that this wealth stimulated our technology and our entire productive system in such a way that we developed an unparalleled aptitude for converting many previously inconvertible materials and sources of power into forms that also constituted wealth. If we were unique in the original heritage, we are not at all unique in the possession of potential assets whose value may be realized by the application of technological skill. Thus we are in position to affirm to the world that, although we are in many respects set apart by our natural plenty, in many other respects we are qualified to show other countries the path that may lead them to a plenty like our own. But we have thrown away this opportunity by failing to display the processes which others might emulate and by showing, instead, the end-product—our standard of living—which they can only envy. Then we have deepened the alienation by blaming other peoples for failing to embrace the political ideals which our standard of living supports.

In spite of the early export of such American technological devices as the McCormick reaper and in spite of attempts, through the Point Four program, to stimulate production in undeveloped countries, it remains painfully true that we have urged other nations to adopt our democracy as their own, while encouraging them to draw upon our abundance in such a way (by the importation of consumer goods) that it remains distinctively our own. Democracy has been held up as a matter of political morality, involving privileges of citizenship which mean little to people below a certain economic level, and it has not been presented as a highly flexible social system conducive to the economic energy and growth which provide abundance. Abundance has been presented as an entirely separate feature of American life and has been manifested to the world primarily in the form of consumer goods which excite the international envy of those whose needs they satisfy, without in any way removing either the sources of envy or the sources of need.[5] Consequently, America's abundance has probably done more to cut us off from actual moral leadership than it has done to enhance such leadership. And certainly it has placed American generosity—much of which is both genuine and unselfish—under the curse of chronic envy.

As a result, our message to the world has become involved in a dilemma: to other peoples, our democracy has seemed attainable but not especially desirable; our abundance has seemed infinitely desirable but quite unattainable. But, if the realities of the relationship between democracy and abundance had been understood by people of other countries or, what is more to the point, by those Americans who were seeking to impart our message, our democracy would have seemed more desirable, and our abundance would have seemed more attainable. Both these changes would have had the effect of strengthening the moral influence of the United States.

In this brief consideration of a tremendously complex subject which has challenged all the skill of large staffs of trained workers in our government, there is no intention to imply that a simple and easy solution for international difficulties lies ready at hand. Nor would I suggest that these workers have universally lacked insight into the relationship between democracy and abundance.

5. Robert Trumbull, writing from India, in the *New York Times*, August 28, 1950, said: "United States propaganda here dwells too much on the success of individualistic method and not enough on the method itself."

But, in so far as they may have possessed such insight, certainly they must have been hindered by the general lack of understanding of this matter both at home and abroad. We have talked so much about "free enterprise" as if we just meant laissez faire economics (which all too often is what we did mean) and so much about "democracy" as if we meant some vague, yearning fraternalism (which, again, is too often what we did mean) that we have failed to make the point that democracy paced the growth of our abundance and abundance broadened the base of our democracy.

Thus our whole conception of our mission in the world was distorted by our failure to understand what the world regarded as most significant in our development and what the essential conditions of democratic life in the American sense really are. The factor of abundance, which we first discovered as an environmental condition and which we then converted by technological change into a cultural as well as a physical force, has not only influenced all the aspects of American life in a fundamental way but has also impinged upon our relations with the peoples of the world, and our failure to realize the nature of the relationship between this abundance and our democracy has played a critical part in frustrating our attempts to fulfil the mission of America.

VII. Abundance and the Frontier Hypothesis

Throughout this study, I have attempted to give full attention to the behavioral sciences and their treatment of national character. Their use of the personality-and-culture concept and their analytical approach to many of the related problems has given them a central place in the development of the subject. This is so conspicuously true that, in general, I have treated history as offering an instrument to round out and reinforce their analysis, rather than as offering an alternative means of accounting for national character. Yet no historian can overlook the fact that American history has long provided a classic formula for defining and explaining the American character: this is Frederick Jackson Turner's frontier hypothesis. In any appraisal of what history has to contribute, therefore, it is inevitable that we should return ultimately to the Turner theory. And in any evaluation of the factor of abundance, it is vital to establish what relation, if any, existed between the frontier influence specifically and the general influence of economic abundance. Thus I find myself coming around at last, as all American historians do sooner or later, to that much-debated formulation which the young professor from Wisconsin proposed to the sages of the American Historical Association when they met at Chicago in 1893.

Turner's paper on "The Significance of the Frontier in American History" was not only a turning point in the development of American historical writing; it was also, in the most explicit sense, an explanation of American character, and might, with perfect validity, have been entitled "The Influence of the Frontier on American Character." Passages throughout the essay may be cited to justify this assertion. For instance, Turner declared that, on the frontier, the "perennial rebirth" of society, the "fluidity of American life, this expansion westward with its new opportunities, its continuous touch with the simplicity of primitive society furnish the forces dominating American character." And, again, "to the frontier, the American intellect owes its striking characteristics."[1]

In any analysis of American character, therefore, Turner and his ideas must be considered with the utmost care. Fortunately, this does not mean that we need undertake any general critique of the entire body of Turner's thought. That is a broad field which has been traversed repeatedly by opposing critics—with Avery O. Craven, Joseph Schafer, and Frederic L. Paxson guarding the essential points of the Turner position and with a number of writers, including Charles A. Beard, Louis Hacker, Fred A. Shannon, James C. Malin, Carlton J. H. Hayes, Murray Kane, Benjamin F. Wright, Jr., and Carter Goodrich in collaboration with Sol Davidson, conducting the assault on specific sectors, while George Wilson Pierson, in a series of articles, has provided a very searching analysis and review of the entire question.[2]

But, in so far as the frontier hypothesis is related to the factor of abundance, it behooves us to take account of it here; and, in fact, it is intimately related. Turner himself said, "the Western wilds, from the Alleghanies to the Pacific, constituted the richest free gift that was ever spread out before civilized man. . . . Never

1. All quotations from Turner, except where otherwise noted, are taken from "The Significance of the Frontier in American History," using the revised form which appeared in his *The Frontier in American History* (New York: Henry Holt & Co., 1920).

2. For a bibliography of this literature, with reference not only to the controversial writers, but also to studies of Turner's precursors, his influence, his thought, and his method, by Herman C. Nixon, Everett E. Edwards, Fulmer Mood, and Merle Curti, respectively, see Ray Allen Billington, *Westward Expansion* (New York: Macmillan Co., 1949), pp. 760–61.

again can such an opportunity come to the sons of men."[3] And, specifically linking this opportunity with the frontier, he added, "The most significant thing about the American frontier is that it lies at the hither edge of free land."

Of course, it should be recognized at once that Turner conceived of other factors besides abundance as being present in the frontier condition. To name only two, there was a temporary lowering of civilized standards, and there was a weakening of the power of traditional institutions such as church and school, with a corresponding enhancement of the stature of the individual.

Therefore we are dealing with abundance as one in a complex of factors, and it becomes important to determine, as far as we can, how much of the influence of what Turner called the "frontier" lay in its being on the outskirts of civilization and how much lay in its function as the locus of maximum access to unused resources. The question is a critical one because, if the factor of abundance was really primary, if the most significant thing about the frontier was, as Turner himself asserted, its contiguity to free land, then we ought to recognize the primacy of abundance and speak of the influence of abundance, in whatever form it occurs, and not restrictively in only one of its manifestations—the frontier manifestation. Do we really mean the influence of the frontier, or do we mean the influence of a factor that was especially conspicuous in the frontier situation but that also operated apart from it upon many other parts of American experience?[4] In so far as the latter is what we mean, we might justifiably

3. "Contributions of the West to American Democracy," in *The Frontier in American History*, p. 261.

4. "To Turner, however, 'the most significant thing about the American frontier' is not that historically it represents a vast domain of natural resources ready to be transformed into capital through the medium of the productive process, but that it lies geographically at the 'hither edge of free land'" (Murray Kane, "Some Considerations on the Frontier Concept of Frederick Jackson Turner," *Mississippi Valley Historical Review*, XXVII [1940], 389).

"One of the major deficiences of the Turner approach was the failure

regard Turner's famous paper as being, in essence, a study of the significance of economic abundance in American history.

In grappling with this problem, we cannot expect, unfortunately, to secure as much precise guidance as we might wish from an analysis of Turner's own writings. His conception of the frontier was nothing if not a protean one. Sometimes he seems to think of the frontier as a geographical region, as when he says that "the Western wilds from the Alleghanies to the Pacific" were the special area where nature conferred a unique bounty or that a new order of Americanism emerged when "the mountains rose between the pioneer and the seaboard." Sometimes he conceives of a condition, the existence at the edge of settlement of an unused area of free land. In this sense the frontier becomes, as Dixon Ryan Fox said, simply "the edge of the unused." Sometimes, again, he conceives of it as a process: "The peculiarity of American institutions is the fact that they have been compelled to adapt themselves to the changes of an expanding people—to the changes involved in crossing a continent, in winning a wilderness, and in developing at each area of this progress out of the primitive economic and political conditions of the frontier into the complexity of city life." Avery O. Craven has summarized this idea of process very effectively in a paraphrase of the concept as he construes it: "The basic idea . . . was that American history, through most of its course, presents a series of recurring social evolutions in diverse geographical areas as a people advance to colonize a continent. The chief characteristic is expansion; the chief peculiarity of institutions, constant readjustment. . . . Into . . . raw and differing areas men and institutions and ideas poured from older basins, there to return to a more or less primitive state and then to climb slowly back toward complexity. . . . The

---

to see that free raw materials stood in almost exactly the same relation to the opportunity for industrial urbanism as the hither edge of free land did to agriculture" (James C. Malin, "Mobility and History," *Agricultural History*, XVII [1943], 178).

process was similar in each case, with some common results but always with 'essential differences' due to time and place."[5]

Certainly, then, if Turner did not use the term "frontier" to mean various things at various times, at least he used it in a way that placed heavy stress first on one aspect, then on another, with very little notice to the reader that the cluster of ideas back of the term was being substantially changed. No doubt he was right in the view that a whole complex of factors was associated with the westward advance of settlement and that all these factors ought to be taken into account. But his technique, very frustrating to many critics of the last two decades, was instead of treating the separate constituents as separate constituents, to fuse all and discuss them interchangeably under the rubric "frontier." George Wilson Pierson, who has made a careful analysis of this shifting concept, remarks ruefully that, to Turner, "the West was rough (a geographic factor) and it was empty (a sociological force). Perhaps, then, Turner's greatest achievement was his successful marriage of these two dissimilar forces in the single phrase, *free land*."[6]

The real key, however, to Turner's thought—both in its strength and in its limitations—will never be grasped if we suppose that this elusiveness of definition was simply the result of a vagueness of mind or an indifference to analysis. It is rather, as Henry Nash Smith has recently argued, the result of Turner's personal predilection for one special social ideal—the ideal of agrarian democracy. As Smith expresses this, "from the time of Franklin down to the end of the frontier period almost a century and a half later, the West had been a constant reminder of the importance of agriculture in American society. It had nourished an agrarian philosophy and an agrarian myth that purported to set forth the character and destinies of the nation. The

5. "Frederick Jackson Turner," in William T. Hutchinson (ed.), *Marcus W. Jernegan Essays in American Historiography* (Chicago: University of Chicago Press, 1937), p. 254.

6. George Wilson Pierson, "The Frontier and American Institutions," *New England Quarterly*, XV (1942), 252.

philosophy and the myth affirmed an admirable set of values, but they ceased very early to be useful in interpreting American society as a whole, because they offered no intellectual apparatus for taking account of the industrial revolution. A system which revolved about a half-mystical conception of nature and held up as an ideal a rudimentary type of agriculture was powerless to confront issues arising from the advance of technology. Agrarian theory encouraged men to ignore the industrial revolution altogether, or to regard it as an unfortunate and anomalous violation of the natural order of things. In the . . . sphere of historical scholarship, for example, the agrarian emphasis of the frontier hypothesis has tended to divert attention from the problems created by industrialization for a half-century during which the United States has become the most powerful industrial nation in the world." Turner's "problem"—the one that he set for himself—was "to find a basis for democracy in some aspect of civilization as he observed it about him in the United States. His determined effort in this direction showed that his mind and his standards of social ethics were subtler and broader than the conceptual system within which the frontier hypothesis had been developed, but he was the prisoner of the assumptions he had taken over from the agrarian tradition."[7]

Applying this dictum specifically to the factor of abundance, one can readily verify Smith's general observations. What happened was that, when abundance operated within an agrarian context—in the form of free land for farmers—Turner seized upon it, but with a tendency to identify the factor with the context, to attribute to the context the results that followed from the operation of the factor, while refusing to recognize the operation of the factor when it occurred outside the selected context.[8]

7. Henry Nash Smith, *Virgin Land* (Cambridge, Mass.: Harvard University Press, 1950), pp. 258–59.

8. "Absorption in the Turner philosophy, centering around agriculture, seems to have diverted attention from the significant and all-important fact that there was still opportunity, created by the fluidity of society based on the industrial urbanism" (Malin, *loc. cit.*).

In this connection it would be misleading to say that Turner refused to admit the existence of nonagrarian frontiers. On the contrary, he mentioned them explicitly and specified also that various frontiers offered various conditions and inducements. In his own words, "the unequal rate of advance compels us to distinguish the frontier into the trader's frontier, the rancher's frontier, or the miner's frontier, and the farmer's frontier."

But, although these dissimilarities forced him grudgingly—"compelled" him, in his own revealing phrase—to give formal recognition to a variety of frontiers, they conspicuously failed to compel him to broaden his concept of the frontier sufficiently to accommodate them. When he came to such matters as the exploitation of salt, coal, oil, and other mineral resources, he would neither separate them out, thus conceding the limitations of his agrarian hypothesis, nor include them actively in his calculations, thus modifying and qualifying the agrarian tenor of his theme.

The arbitrary restrictiveness of this agrarian preoccupation is shown very clearly, it seems to me, in a statement by Carl Becker, who was one of Turner's most brilliant and most faithful followers. Becker said, "The United States has always had, until very recently, more land that it could use and fewer people than it needed." Certainly this premise would be difficult to refute. Then he continues: "This is not only the fundamental economic difference between the United States and European countries, but it is a condition which has more influence than any other in determining the course of American history."[9] Today the United States has, perhaps, as large an industrial capacity as the rest of the world, and it was well on the way to such leadership when Becker wrote; yet the factor which he offers as the key to the fundamental economic difference between America and the Old World turns its back upon this major development

---

9. *The United States: An Experiment in Democracy* (New York: Harper & Bros., 1920), p. 143.

of our economic life. Clearly, it is not merely the greater endowment of land which has differentiated America's growth from Europe's. It is the greater supply, also, of timber, of iron, of copper, of petroleum, of coal, of hydroelectric power. By some mystic process these may be subsumed under the term "land," but if we should speak of land in this sense, as meaning everything except sea and air, we ought at least to recognize that it is in this form too broad for the agrarians to claim a franchise on it. Indeed, it then becomes more nearly equivalent to physical abundance, or at least potential physical abundance, than to soil.

Because of these anomalies and because of the presence of concealed agrarian dogma in what purports to be an environmental analysis, it becomes important to consider a little more closely what the elements were in the frontier situation as Turner conceived it. I have already suggested that he was by no means schematic in his approach to this question, but I think we may agree in identifying his major points of stress. As I have already observed, he constantly recurred to the factor of plenty in the form of free land. Sometimes he touched this theme as a lyric chord, as when he said "American democracy was born of no theorist's dream; it was not carried in the *Susan Constant* to Virginia, nor in the *Mayflower* to Plymouth. It came out of the American forest, and it gained new strength each time it touched a new frontier. Not the Constitution, but free land and an abundance of natural resources open to a fit people, made the democratic type of society in America for three centuries."[10] Sometimes he dealt with the same thought in more analytical economic terms, as when he explained the precise motives that stimulated the westward push: "The farmers [of settled areas] who lived on soil whose returns were diminished by unrotated crops were offered the virgin soil of the frontier at nominal prices. Their growing families demanded more lands, and these were

10. "The West and American Ideals," in *The Frontier in American History*, p. 293.

dear. The competition of the unexhausted, cheap, and easily tilled prairie lands compelled the farmer either to go west and continue the exhaustion of the soil on a new frontier, or to adopt intensive culture. Thus the census of 1890 shows, in the Northwest, many counties in which there is an absolute or a relative decrease of population. These states have been sending farmers to advance the frontier on the plains and have themselves begun to turn to intensive farming and to manufacture." But, whether in didactic or in poetic terms, Turner reiterated constantly the factor of abundance, which he recognized most frequently, but not invariably, in the form of land.

Another feature of the frontier which Turner consistently emphasized as important was the fact that it temporarily emancipated the individual from institutional controls. Often though he returned to this point, it seems to me that he never did develop it with real clarity; but there is one formulation of the idea in his statement that "we have the complex European life sharply precipitated by the wilderness into the simplicity of primitive conditions." This, I take it, means two things: It means that the system of division of labor, prevalent in complex societies, breaks down, and the individual is obliged to diversify his activities—to produce his own food, to minister to his own soul, to educate his own children, to doctor his own ailments, to provide his own police protection, and to be a true self-sufficing man. It means also that, since he, as an individual, has gone ahead of organized society, leaving it to follow him, he is not overshadowed by the weight of institutions, and his stature as an individual is correspondingly greater.

Another factor that Turner regarded as intrinsic was the way in which the frontier dictated a temporary lowering of the standards of civilization. The pioneers, of course, accepted this regression only because they expected it to pay off in a raising of standards later; but for the first phase, at least, there was an inescapable reduction: "The wilderness masters the colonist. . . .

It strips off the garments of civilization and arrays him in the hunting shirt and the moccasin. It puts him in the log cabin of the Cherokee and Iroquois and runs an Indian palisade around him. Before long he has gone to planting Indian corn and plowing with a sharp stick; he shouts the war cry and takes the scalp in orthodox Indian fashion."

It is difficult to be certain whether or not Turner viewed this change with a romantic primitivism that caused him to take pleasure in it; but in any case he certainly regarded it as the most transitory of conditions. Frederic L. Paxson, paraphrasing Turner, expresses the concept well when he says that "as the pioneer trudged ahead of his little procession, along the rugged trails that pierced the mountain gaps, he was only incidentally living in the present. The future filled his mind; a future beginning with the rough shack that must shelter him for his first season; but a future of field after field of fertile land, of houses and livestock, of growing family and the education and religion that it needed."[11]

Along with these factors there was also, as I have suggested previously, the element of successive readjustments, of "perennial rebirth," of constant changes moving in a kind of rhythmic cycle, "the changes involved in crossing a continent, in winning a wilderness, and in developing at each area of this progress out of the primitive economic and political conditions of the frontier into the complexity of city life." Always, of course, this cycle was a democratic one.

Most of the things which the frontier meant to Turner are embraced, I believe, by one or another of these factors. It was the place where free land lay at the edge of settlement; the place where institutions no longer towered over the individual man; the place where European complexity gave way to American simplicity; and the place where democratic growth and change

11. *When the West Is Gone* (New York: Henry Holt & Co., 1930), p. 39.

was repeatedly re-enacted as a process and reaffirmed as a principle.

But how did these elements in the pioneer experience impinge upon the American character? What was their influence in shaping the traits of the American people? Here Turner's analysis is somewhat more explicit, and it is, in fact, easier to know what he meant by the "influence of the frontier" than what he meant by the "frontier" itself. First of all, he was confident that the frontier promoted nationalism: the pioneer looked to the national government to adopt the measures he needed—to provide him with internal improvements, to administer the public domain, and still more to accord to the area in which he had settled territorial status and, later, statehood; moreover, the pioneer, on the frontier, mingled with other settlers from other states and even from other countries. Here was the true melting pot, and "on the tide of the Father of Waters, North and South met and mingled into a nation." "It was," he said, "this nationalizing tendency of the West that transformed the democracy of Jefferson into the national republicanism of Monroe and the democracy of Andrew Jackson. The West of the War of 1812, the West of Clay and Benton and Harrison and Andrew Jackson, shut off by the Middle States and the mountains from the coast sections, had a solidarity of its own with national tendencies." Second, he was equally confident that the frontier had fostered democracy: "The most important effect of the frontier has been in the promotion of democracy here and in Europe." In this connection Turner often cited the liberal suffrage provisions with which the frontier states came into the Union and the reactive effects of these provisions upon the political arrangements in the older states. Third, he also credited the frontier with stimulating the spirit of individualism: "Complex society," he felt, "is precipitated by the wilderness into a kind of primitive organization based on the family. The tendency is anti-social. It produces antipathy to control." And with each family occupying land of its own, very largely on a self-sufficing basis, there was, in fact, every reason why the individual should feel a minimum need to be cared for by society, and therefore a minimum tolerance for control by society. This was true only on the farmer's frontier, of course, and Turner himself recognized that other frontiers might not be individualistic at all. He himself stated this limitation, saying, "But when the arid lands and the mineral resources of the Far West were reached, no conquest was possible by the old individual pioneer methods. Here expensive irrigation works must be constructed, coöperative activity was demanded in utilization of the water supply, capital beyond the reach of the small farmer was required. In a word, the physiographic province itself decreed that the destiny of this new frontier should be social rather than individual."[12] But, as was characteristic with him, though he might give lip service to the existence of a variety of frontiers, it always turned out that the farmer's frontier was the one he was really talking about, and the others lay somewhere beyond the periphery of his thought. And the farmer's frontier was unquestionably individualistic. Thus he did not hesitate to rank individualism with his other factors and to declare that the "frontier of settlement . . . carried with it individualism, democracy, and nationalism."

These three were, in a sense, his triad—factors to which he often recurred. But however important they may be and however deeply they may be imbedded in the character, they can hardly be described as "traits of character" or "qualities of mind" in the ordinary sense; and we must therefore go one step further, to ask: How did Turner conceive that the frontier made the pioneer unlike other people? The complete answer, of course, runs through the whole body of his work, but there is a very good summary answer near the end of his famous essay. "To the frontier," he said, "the American intellect owes its striking

12. "Contributions of the West to American Democracy," in *The Frontier in American History*, p. 258.

characteristics. That coarseness and strength combined with acuteness and inquisitiveness; that practical, inventive turn of mind, quick to find expedients; that masterful grasp of material things, lacking in the artistic but powerful to effect great ends; that restless, nervous energy; that dominant individualism, working for good and for evil, and withal that buoyancy and exuberance which comes with freedom—these are traits of the frontier, or traits called out elsewhere because of the existence of the frontier."

Such, then, were the main elements of the frontier hypothesis, as Turner developed it: West of the Alleghenies lay a vast expanse of fertile and unsettled land which became available almost free to those who would cultivate it. Across this area, a frontier or edge of settlement pushed steadily west, and along this frontier individuals who had advanced ahead of society's usual institutional controls accepted a lowering of standards at the time for the sake of progress in the future. Constantly repeating over again a democratic experience, they reinforced the national democratic tradition. All these conditions, of course, influenced the mental traits of those who were directly or indirectly involved in the process, and especially their nationalism, their democracy, and their individualism were stimulated. Certain other qualities—a coarseness, combined with a strength, a practicality and materialism of mind, a restless energy, and a measure of buoyancy or exuberance—were all traceable to this frontier influence.

With this outline of the frontier hypothesis in mind, we can now revert to the question: To what extent was the frontier merely the context in which abundance occurred? To what extent does it explain developments which the concept of abundance alone could not explain?

At times Turner himself seemed almost to equate the frontier with abundance, as, for instance, when he said, "These free lands promoted individualism, economic equality, freedom to rise, democracy."[13] It is probably valid to criticize him for this. But if there was a fallacy in his failure to distinguish between these coinciding factors and his consequent practice of treating qualities which were intrinsically derived from abundance as if they were distinctive to the frontier, it would be the same fallacy in reverse to treat qualities which were intrinsically frontier qualities as if they were attributable to abundance. Bearing this caveat in mind, we can hardly deny that there were a number of influences which were peculiar to the frontier or to abundance in its distinctive frontier form and which did not operate outside the frontier phase. For instance, the pioneer's necessity of submitting to hardships and low living standards as the price of higher standards later must certainly have stimulated his optimism and his belief in progress. Similarly, one can hardly doubt that the mingling of peoples on the frontier and their urgent need for federal legislative measures must have stimulated the growth of nationalism just as Turner said. And again, at an even deeper level, it is hard to doubt that the frontier projection of the individual ahead of society and the self-sufficing way of life on the edge of settlement must have greatly stimulated American individualism.

But even to say that Turner was right in all these matters is not to say that he took a comprehensive view of the American experience. By confining his explanation of Americanism to the conditions of the pioneer stage of our development, he placed himself in the position of implying that nothing distinctively American would be left, except as a residue, after the pioneer stage had been passed. By limiting his recognition of abundance to its appearance in the form of free land, he limited his recognition of successive American democratic readjustments to the successive settlement of new areas of free land, and thus he cut himself off from a recognition of the adjustments to technological advance, to urban growth, and to the higher standard of

13. *Ibid.*, p. 259.

living, all of which have contributed quite as much as the frontier to the fluidity and facility for change in American life. Further, by failing to recognize that the frontier was only one form in which America offered abundance, he cut himself off from an insight into the fact that other forms of abundance had superseded the frontier even before the supply of free land had been exhausted, with the result that it was not really the end of free land but rather the substitution of new forms of economic activity which terminated the frontier phase of our history.

Perhaps it may be in order to say a few words more about each of these points. In the first place, then, by making the frontier the one great hopeful factor in our experience, Turner gave us every cause to feel alarm and pessimism about the conditions that would follow the disappearance of the frontier. As he himself expressed it, "since the days when the fleet of Columbus sailed into the waters of the New World, America has been another name for opportunity. . . . He would be a rash prophet who should assert that the expansive character of American life has now entirely ceased. Movement has been its dominant fact, and, unless this training has no effect upon a people, the American energy will continually demand a wider field for its exercise. But never again will such gifts of free land offer themselves. . . . Now, four centuries from the discovery of America, at the end of a hundred years of life under the Constitution, the frontier has gone, and with its going has closed the first period of American history."

The tone of foreboding in this statement is easily transformed into a defeatist lament or into a conviction that, without the frontier, freedom and opportunity are endangered. To take but one of a good many possible illustrations, Governor Philip La Follette, in his message to the Wisconsin legislature in 1931, observed that "in the days of our pioneer fathers, the free land of the frontier gave this guarantee of freedom and opportunity," but that no such natural safeguard remained in operation after the passing of the frontier.[14]

Some years ago Dixon Ryan Fox pointed out this defeatist corollary of the frontier hypothesis and suggested that broader definition of a frontier which I have already mentioned—namely, "the edge of the unused." This would imply, of course, that science has its frontiers, industry its frontiers, technology its frontiers, and that so long as Americans can advance their standards of living and maintain the fluidity of their lives and their capacity for change along these frontiers, the disappearance of the agrarian frontier is not at all critical. In terms of abundance, Turner was correct in saying, "Never again will such gifts of free land offer themselves," but his implication that nature would never again offer such bounty is open to challenge, for the frontiers of industry, of invention, and of engineering have continued to bring into play new resources quite as rich as the unbroken sod of the western frontier.

A second point which I believe Turner's agrarian orientation caused him to overlook was the broad variety of factors which have worked to cause unceasing change and development in America and thereby have conditioned the American to a habit of constant adjustment, constant adaptation to new circumstances, and constant readiness to accept or experiment with what is new. It was "to the frontier" that he attributed "that practical inventive turn of mind, quick to find expedients," to it that he credited the fact that Americans were "compelled to

14. James C. Malin observes that the doctrine of closed space caused "the hysterical conservation movement of the early twentieth century. It remained for the apologists of the New Deal, however, and especially such men as Rexford G. Tugwell and Henry A. Wallace [author of *New Frontiers*], to invoke in extreme form the prestige of the Turner tradition to justify governmental regulation of American life as a substitute for the vanished frontier. . . . In effect it was a repudiation of the America of Turner, accompanied by the application of an unwanted corollary from his own teaching" (*op. cit.*, p. 177).

adapt themselves to the changes of an expanding people." But clearly it is not "the simplicity of primitive society" which requires new expedients and inventive ability; on the contrary, primitive society was highly repetitive in its patterns and demanded stamina more than talent for innovation; it was an increasingly complex society of rapid technological change, far away from the frontier, which demanded range and flexibility of adjustment. No amount of concentration upon the frontier will give us an awareness of the way in which the American home has been readjusted to the use first of gas and later of electricity; of the way in which American business has been readjusted to the typewriter and the comptometer; of the way in which American communication has been adjusted to the telegraph, the telephone, the radio, and even the motion picture; and of the way in which the American community has been readjusted to the railroad, the streetcar, and the automobile. One has only to compare an old, preautomobile city, like Boston, with a new, postautomobile city, like Houston, Texas, with its supermarkets, its drive-in restaurants, and its other facilities for automotive living, to appreciate that this is true. Are not these constant changes more important in maintaining the fluidity of American life, in perpetuating the habit of expecting something different, than any number of successive removals to new areas of free land?

A third and final aspect in which the agrarian perspective proved too limiting is in the fact that Turner did not recognize that the attraction of the frontier was simply as the most accessible form of abundance, and therefore he could not conceive that other forms of abundance might replace it as the lodestone to which the needle of American aspirations would point. To him the frontier remained the polar force until it was exhausted; America must turn to second-best resources after this unparalleled opportunity of the frontier had passed. Yet, in fact, what happened was that, as early as the mid-century, if not earlier, American industrial growth, relying upon the use of other forms of abundance than soil fertility, began to compete with the frontier in the opportunities which it offered, and the migration of Americans began to point to the cities rather than to the West.[15] Later, this same industrial growth provided a general standard of living so high that people were no longer willing to abandon it for the sake of what the frontier promised. This can be stated almost in the terms of a formula: The frontier, with its necessity for some reduction of living standards, could attract people from settled areas so long as the existing standards in those areas did not exceed a certain maximum (people would accept a certain unfavorable differential in their current standards for the sake of potential gain). But when existing city standards exceeded this maximum, when the differential became too great, people would no longer accept it even for all the future rewards that the frontier might promise. To leave a primitive agrarian community and settle in primitive agrarian isolation was one thing, but to leave refrigeration, electric lighting, running water, hospitals, motion pictures, and access to highways was another, and, as these amenities and others like them were introduced, the frontier distinctly lost the universality of its lure. As George W. Pierson says, "When cars, movies, and radios become essentials of the accepted standard of living, subsistence farming is repugnant even to the starving. Measured, therefore, against this concept of a changing fashion or standard of living, it may be suggested that the lure of the land began in Tudor England before there was any available, and ceased in the United States before the available supply gave out."[16] In short, the frontier ceased to operate as a major force in American history not when it disappeared—not when the superintendent of the census aban-

15. Walter P. Webb, *The Great Frontier* (Boston: Houghton Mifflin Co., 1952), p. 374, quotes Carl, in John Steinbeck's "The Red Pony" (1945), "No, no place to go, Jody. Every place is taken. But that's not the worst—no, not the worst. Westering has died out of the people. Westering isn't a hunger any more. It's all done."

16. *Op. cit.*, p. 239.

doned the attempt to map a frontier boundary—but when the primary means of access to abundance passed from the frontier to other focuses in American life.

It is now sixty years since Turner wrote his famous essay. For two-thirds of this period his ideas commanded vast influence and indiscriminate acceptance, and then they encountered a barrage of criticism as severe as it was belated. Some aspects of his thought have received such devastating analysis that no historian today would be likely to make the error of adopting them. For instance, historians today would be wary of the agrarian assumptions in Turner's formulation. But the geographical determinism or environmentalism of Turner still possesses great vitality. The strength of its appeal was demonstrated again in 1952 more strikingly, perhaps, than ever before in this country, with the publication by Walter P. Webb of another and a broader restatement of the frontier hypothesis—not for the United States alone, this time, but for the entire planet.

Webb's *Great Frontier* cuts free of both the restrictive Americanism and the restrictive agrarianism of Turner to propose the thesis that the world frontier, opened up by the age of discovery, was "inherently a vast body of wealth without proprietors," that it precipitated a "sudden, continuing, and ever-increasing flood of wealth" upon the centers of Western civilization, thus inaugurating a period of boom which lasted about four hundred years and during which all the institutions—economic, political, and social—evolved to meet the needs of a world in boom.

In his explicit recognition that the very essence of the frontier was its supply of unappropriated wealth, Webb has clarified a vital factor which remained obscure in Turner, for Turner seemed to sense the point without clearly stating it, and Turner always neglected forms of wealth other than soil fertility. Webb, with his attention to the precious metals and even more with his focus upon the importance of "that form of wealth classed as

Things or commodities," everlastingly breaks the link between agrarian thought and the frontier doctrine. Through his clear perception of the part played by abundance, he has demonstrated in thorough and convincing fashion the validity of the precise point which I have attempted to put forward in this analysis.

If it were only a question whether the frontier has significance intrinsically as a locus of wealth, therefore, my comment would be only to echo Professor Webb; but there is another question: whether the *only* significant source of modern wealth is the frontier. Webb seems to contend that it is, for he asserts that "it was the constant distribution on a nominal or free basis of the royal or public domain that kept the boom going and that gave a peculiar dynamic quality to Western civilization for four centuries,"[17] and his discussion is pervaded with dark forebodings for the future of a world which no longer commands such a stock of untapped resources.

The present study has been built, in large part, upon the theme of American abundance, which is, of course, New World abundance and therefore, in large measure, frontier abundance. This theme is, in many respects, fully in accord with Professor Webb's and at first glance might appear identical with it. But, at the point where Webb attributes to the frontier an exclusive function, my argument diverges from his. In chapter iii, I have already sought to show that American abundance has been in part freely supplied by the bounty of nature, but also that it has been in part socially created by an advancing technology, and that neither of these factors can explain modern society without the other. Abundance, as a horse-breeder might say, is by technology out of environment. Professor Webb has treated the subject as if environment bred abundance by spontaneous generation.

To approach the matter more explicitly, let us consider the basis of our present standard of living, which reflects the supply

17. *Op. cit.,* p. 413.

of goods of all kinds. This standard results not merely from our stock of resources, for primitive peoples with bare subsistence standards have possessed the same resources for as long as fifty thousand years. It results also from our ability to convert these resources into socially useful form—that is, from our productive capacity. Our productive capacity, in turn, depends not only on the raw materials, which are ready to hand, but even more upon our ability to increase, through mechanization, the volume of goods which can be turned out by each worker. If I may allude again to a previously used illustration, an infinite supply of free land would never, by itself, have raised our standard of living very far, for it would never have freed us from the condition in which more than 70 per cent of our labor force was required to produce food for our population. But, when technology enabled 11 per cent of our labor force to produce food for our population, it freed 60 per cent to engage in other activities—that is, to create other goods which would become part of the standard of living.

No doubt it is true that in many societies the level of living will be controlled by the scarcity of resources (e.g., by lack of soil fertility), and certainly there is good reason to feel concern lest such controls should come into play in the future as world population multiplies and world resources are expended. But in most of the societies with which history has had to deal, it was the limited productivity of the worker rather than the absolute lack of resources in the environment which fixed the maximum level for the standard of living. In these societies where technology has been the limiting factor, it would clearly be fallacious to seek the explanation for an increase of wealth solely in the increasing supply of resources, since the society already possessed resources which it was not using.

In practice, however, the forces of technology and environment constantly interact and cannot be isolated. Because they do interact, it might be argued, with some force, that the richness of supply of resources has stimulated the technology—that the spectacle of vast riches waiting to be grasped has inspired men to devise new means for grasping them—and that, in this sense, the great frontier precipitated the new technology. But, without denying either the attractiveness of, or the elements of truth in, such an interpretation, which would buttress the Webb thesis, I think we should recognize that historically the technological revolution seemed to precede the age of discovery. From the time of the Crusades, four centuries before Columbus and Da Gama, western Europe was in transition. The use of gunpowder, the art of printing, improvements in navigation, the revival of commerce, the development of various sciences, and the whole pervasive change known as the Renaissance—all these had paved the way not only for the great geographical discoveries but also for the industrial transformation of Europe. Viewing the matter in this way, it might be argued that what really happened was that an advancing technology opened up a whole new range of potentialities, including the physical resources of the New World, rather than that the epic geographical discoveries called into being a new technology.

Probably it is as fruitless to seek the dynamics of economic change solely in technology as it is to seek them solely in environment. Certainly nothing would be gained by minimizing the environmental factor, and it is not my purpose to assert either that technology can operate without materials or that Webb's Malthusian concern for the future is unjustified. But precisely because the factor of abundance is of capital significance, it is important that it should not become identified with doctrines of geographical determinism. And precisely because Webb's formulation is one of the first fully developed treatments of this factor, it is unfortunate that he should accept geographical determinism as a necessary part of his position. When he rejects what he calls "the Fallacy of New Frontiers," he is not only attacking a glib and overworked slogan, but he is also attacking the belief that science may find new potentialities in physical materials that are currently regarded as valueless—something which science has repeatedly done in the past. When he asserts that "science can do much, but . . . it is not likely soon to find a new world or make the one we have much better than it is," he offers two propositions of very unequal tenor: the prospect of science's finding a new world is indeed remote, but the entire history of science for several centuries would justify our expectation that, if not perverted to the uses of war, it may make our world a great deal better.

If abundance is to be properly understood, it must not be visualized in terms of a storehouse of fixed and universally recognizable assets, reposing on shelves until humanity, by a process of removal, strips all the shelves bare. Rather, abundance resides in a series of physical potentialities, which have never been inventoried at the same value for any two cultures in the past and are not likely to seem of identical worth to different cultures in the future. As recently as twenty years ago, for example, society would not have counted uranium among its important assets. When abundance exercises a function in the history of man, it is not as an absolute factor in nature to which man, as a relative factor, responds. Rather, it is as a physical and cultural factor, involving the interplay between man, himself a geological force, and nature, which holds different meanings for every different human culture and is therefore relative.

In short, abundance is partly a physical and partly a cultural manifestation. For America, from the eighteenth to the twentieth century, the frontier was the focus of abundance, physically because the land there was virgin and culturally because the Anglo-Americans of that time were particularly apt at exploiting the new country.[18] At this lowest threshold of access to abundance, the pioneers found an individualism and a nationalism which they might not have found at other thresholds. But, though physically the frontier remained the site of virgin land, cultural changes gave to the people an aptitude for exploiting new industrial potentialities and thus drew the focus of abundance away from the frontier. But this change of focus itself perpetuated and reinforced the habits of fluidity, of mobility, of change, of the expectation of progress, which have been regarded as distinctive frontier traits. The way in which this happened suggests that it was, in reality, abundance in any form, including the frontier form, rather than the frontier in any unique sense, which wrought some of the major results in the American experience. The frontier remained of primary significance precisely as long as it remained the lowest threshold of access to America's abundance; it ceased to be primary when other thresholds were made lower, and not when the edge of unsettled land ceased to exist. American abundance, by contrast, has remained of primary significance both in the frontier phase and in the vast industrial phase which has dominated American life for the past three-quarters of a century. American development and the American character are too complex to be explained by any single factor, but, among the many factors which do have to be taken into account, it is questionable whether any has exerted a more formative or more pervasive influence than the large measure of economic abundance which has been so constantly in evidence.

18. Pierson asks, "What about the Spaniards, who had the run of the whole hemisphere? Did the Mississippi Valley make them democratic, prosperous and numerous? In a word, do not the level of culture and the 'fitness' of a society for the wilderness, matter more than the wilderness? . . . If today a new continent were to rise out of the Pacific Ocean, are we so sure that it would encourage small freeholds, not corporation or governmental monopolies?" (*op. cit.*, p. 253).

VIII. The Institution of Abundance: Advertising

For millions of people throughout the world, during the last three centuries, America has symbolized plenty. This profusion of wealth, this abundance of goods, has borne a significance that far transcends the field of economics. American democracy, in the broad sense, was made possible to begin with by a condition of economic surplus, and the constant incidence of this abundance has differentiated American democracy from the democracy of other, less richly endowed countries.

Abundance, then, must be reckoned a major force in our history. But one may question whether any force can be regarded as possessing major historic importance unless it has developed its own characteristic institution. Democracy, for instance, produces the institution of popular government—the whole complex of parties, elections, representative bodies, constitutions, and the like. Religion manifests itself in the church, with a canon law, a clergy, and a whole ecclesiastical system. Science and learning find institutional embodiment in universities, with all their libraries, laboratories, faculties, and other apparatus of scholarship. If abundance can legitimately be regarded as a great historical force, what institution is especially identified with it? Does any such institution exist?

In *The Great Frontier*, Walter Prescott Webb contends that the four-hundred-year boom beginning with the age of discovery profoundly altered all the institutions of Western civilization, and especially that it led to the emergence of laissez faire capitalism. He maintains this view most ably and with great insight, and it would be hard to deny that, in the large sense in which he deals with the subject, laissez faire capitalism is an institution of abundance. It is, however, a modification, profound to be sure, of an earlier capitalism and is not a wholly new institution. If we seek an institution that was brought into being by abundance, without previous existence in any form, and, moreover, an institution which is peculiarly identified with American abundance rather than with abundance throughout Western civilization, we will find it, I believe, in modern American advertising.

Advertising as such is by no means a neglected subject. The excesses of advertising and of advertising men have been a favorite theme for a full quorum of modern satirists, cynics, and Jeremiahs. From the patent-medicine exposés in the early years of the century to the latest version of *The Hucksters,* advertising men have incurred fairly constant attack—their unscrupulous natures and their stomach ulcers being equally celebrated. Since advertising lends itself both to aesthetic criticism and to moral criticism and since humanity is ever ready with views in each of these areas, the flow of opinion has been copious.

But advertising as an institution has suffered almost total neglect. One might read fairly widely in the literature which treats of public opinion, popular culture, and the mass media in the United States without ever learning that advertising now compares with such long-standing institutions as the school and the church in the magnitude of its social influence. It dominates the media, it has vast power in the shaping of popular standards, and it is really one of the very limited group of institutions which exercise social control. Yet analysts of society have largely ignored it. Historians seldom do more than glance at it in their studies of social history, and, when they do, they usually focus attention upon some picturesque or titillating aspect, such as the way in which advertising has reflected or encouraged a new frankness about such previously tabooed subjects as ladies' underwear. Histories of American periodicals and even of the mass media deal with advertising as if it were a side issue. Students of the radio and of the mass-circulation magazines frequently condemn advertising for its conspicuous role, as if it were a mere interloper in a separate, pre-existing, self-contained aesthetic world of actors, musicians, authors, and script-writers; they hardly recognize that advertising created modern American radio and television, transformed the modern newspaper, evoked the modern slick periodical, and remains the vital essence of each of them at the present time. Marconi may have invented the wireless and Henry Luce may have invented the news magazine, but it is advertising that has made both wireless and news magazines what they are in America today. It is as impossible to understand a modern popular writer without understanding advertising as it would be to understand a medieval troubadour without understanding the cult of chivalry, or a nineteenth-century revivalist without understanding evangelical religion.

Before undertaking the consideration of advertising as an institution of social control—an instrument comparable to the school and the church in the extent of its influence upon society—perhaps it would be well to begin by observing something of the institution's growth to its present physical magnitude and financial strength.

A century ago advertising was a very minor form of economic activity, involving relatively small sums of money and playing only a negligible part in the distribution of goods or the formation of consumer habits. It was practiced principally by retail distributors who offered items without the mention of brands. Producers, who regarded the distributors as their market and who had as yet no concept of trying to reach the ultimate consumer, did not advertise at all and did not attempt to signalize their product by a distinctive name or label. Advertising ran heavily toward short prosaic notices like the want ads of today, in which the tone was didactic rather than hortatory or inspirational, and the content was factual. But patent medicines, even at that time, were a conspicuous exception.

Publishers usually assumed that advertisements ought to be

of this nature, and, to protect the position of the small advertiser, some of them refused to accept notices using any type larger
than agate. But, to apply the *New Yorker*'s phrase historically,
there has always been an ad man, and some of the ad men of the
mid-century began to use great numbers of agate-sized letters,
arranging them in the shape of large letters, just as the members
of a college band are sometimes arranged in formation to spell out
the initials of the alma mater. Publishers also correctly assumed
that any considerable number of small, compact advertisements
would lend a deadly monotony to the printed page, and some of
them accordingly limited rather narrowly the amount of advertising that they would accept. In 1874, for instance, *The Youth's
Companion* restricted the quantity of its advertising. As late as
the 1870's, when the Howe Sewing Machine Company offered
$18,000 for the back cover of *Harper's*, it was somewhat astonished to meet with a polite but firm refusal.

But those days are gone forever, and no other phenomenon of
eighty years ago is now more remote. By 1880 advertising had
increased threefold since the Civil War period. By 1900 it stood
at $95,000,000 a year, which marked a tenfold increase over the
amount in 1865. By 1919 it exceeded half a billion dollars, and by
1929 it reached $1,120,000,000. After 1929 it declined because of
the Depression, but by 1951 it had again surpassed all previous
levels and stood at $6,548,000,000 a year.

This immense financial growth reflects a number of vast and
far-reaching changes. To begin with, the physical appearance of
advertising underwent a complete transformation. The small box-
insert ad gave way increasingly to larger spreads, and at last the
full-page advertisement became the dominant form. Daniel Starch
has shown, for instance, that in the 1860's and 1870's the average
advertisement in the *Boston Evening Transcript* and the *New
York Tribune* was about four column-inches, but by 1918 it was
four times this size. In magazines, advertisers in the 1880's used
half-page spaces two and a half times as often as they used full

pages; by 1920 they did so only one-third as often. Before 1890 full-page entries constituted only a fifth of the advertising in magazines; but by 1920 they accounted for nearly half, and today the proportion must easily exceed half. Also, black and white gave way increasingly to color. As early as 1868 the *Galaxy* adopted the practice of using colored inserts, and, though this proved a little too far in advance of the times, it ultimately became standard practice among all large-circulation magazines.

Along with these changes in form went significant changes in the economic interests which advertised. For the first time producers began to perceive the possibilities in general advertising. At an earlier time they had addressed advertising by mail or on other limited bases to the distributors whom they hoped to induce to handle their goods, but they had left it to the distributor to deal with the ultimate consumer. As I have previously observed, they had apparently never conceived of the possibility of manufacturing their product under a distinctive brand name, or of using general advertising to create a consumer demand for their brand and thus of exerting pressure upon the distributor to keep their products in stock. But in the 1880's four pioneer producers began regularly to advertise their brands on a large scale. Significantly, perhaps, three of these were soaps: Sapolio, Pear's, and Ivory; the fourth was Royal Baking Powder. All of them achieved a large growth which was indisputably the result of advertising, and by doing so they demonstrated a truth which other producers were quick to grasp. As early as 1905, *Printer's Ink* proclaimed this new gospel when it declared: "This is a golden age in trade marks—a time when almost any maker of a worthy product can lay down the lines of a demand that will not only grow with years beyond anything that has ever been known before, but will become, in some degree, a monopoly. . . . Everywhere . . . there are opportunities to take the lead in advertising—to replace dozens of mongrel, unknown, unacknowledged makes of a fabric, a dress essential, a food, with a standard trade-marked brand, backed by the national advertising that in itself has come to be a guarantee of worth with the public."

As producers recognized the possibilities of this golden age, their advertising grew until it became primary: almost all so-called "national advertising" in magazines and over large networks is advertising by producers—while advertising by distributors, mostly in newspapers and over local broadcasting stations, has become secondary. The historian of the N. W. Ayer and Son Advertising Agency reports that "in the 'seventies and 'eighties, those who advertised through the Ayer firm were largely retailers and others who sold directly to the public. By 1890 most of these had ceased to use the Ayer agency, and its principal work was the advertising of manufacturers who sold through dealers and retailers but preferred to get control over their ultimate market."[1]

Concurrently, the nature of the appeal which advertising employed was transformed. Producers were no longer trying merely to use advertising as a coupling device between existing market demand and their own supply; rather, they were trying to create a demand. Since the function of advertising had become one of exerting influence rather than one of providing information, the older factual, prosy notice which focused upon the specifications of the commodity now gave way to a more lyrical type of appeal which focused instead upon the desires of the consumer. This change was foreshadowed as early as 1903 by Walter Dill Scott, in an article on "The Psychology of Advertising," which formulated the basic law of the subject so clearly that he deserves to be regarded as the Archimedes, if not the Nostradamus, of the advertising world: "How many advertisers," he asked, "describe a piano so vividly that the reader can hear it? How many food products are so described that the reader can taste the food? . . . How many describe an undergarment so that the reader can feel

1. Ralph M. Hower, *The History of an Advertising Agency: N. W. Ayer & Son at Work, 1869–1949* (Cambridge, Mass.: Harvard University Press, 1949), p. 207.

the pleasant contact with his body? Many advertisers seem never to have thought of this, and make no attempt at such a description." That was in 1903. Today many advertisers seem to have thought of nothing else, and certainly all of them understand that advertising operates more to create wants in the minds of people than to capitalize on wants that are already active.[2]

Inevitably a question arises: Why did this immense growth of advertising take place? To this query each of us might offer responses of his own, but perhaps the most carefully considered answer, at least in terms of economics, is provided by Neil H. Borden in his extremely thorough study of *The Economic Effects of Advertising* (1942). Borden explains this growth partly in terms of the widening economic gap between producers and consumers and the consequently increased need for a medium of communication, and he attributes the growth of large-scale national advertising, with its color, large spreads, and other expensive features, to the growth of big corporations able to pay for such publicity. But in addition to these explanations he adds another very essential one: "The quest for product differentiation became intensified as the industrial system became more mature, and as manufacturers had capacity to produce far beyond existing demand."

In other words, advertising is not badly needed in an economy of scarcity, because total demand is usually equal to or in excess of total supply, and every producer can normally sell as much as he produces. It is when potential supply outstrips demand—that is, when abundance prevails—that advertising begins to fulfil a really essential economic function. In this situation the producer knows that the limitation upon his operations and upon his

2. On the history of advertising in general see Frank S. Presbrey, *The History and Development of Advertising* (Garden City, N.Y.: Doubleday Doran & Co., 1929); Ralph M. Hower, *op. cit.* On advertising in periodicals see Frank Luther Mott, *A History of American Magazines* (3 vols.; Cambridge, Mass.: Harvard University Press, 1930–38). Presbrey's work contains the quotations from *Printer's Ink* and from Walter Dill Scott.

growth no longer lies, as it lay historically, in his productive capacity, for he can always produce as much as the market will absorb; the limitation has shifted to the market, and it is selling capacity which controls his growth. Moreover, every other producer of the same kind of article is also in position to expand output indefinitely, and this means that the advertiser must distinguish his product, if not on essential grounds, then on trivial ones, and that he must drive home this distinction by employing a brand name and by keeping this name always before the public. In a situation of limited supply the scarcity of his product will assure his place in the market, but in a situation of indefinitely expandable supply his brand is his only means of assuring himself of such a place.

Let us consider this, however, not merely from the standpoint of the enterpriser but in terms of society as a whole. At once the vital nature of the change will be apparent: the most critical point in the functioning of society shifts from production to consumption, and, as it does so, the culture must be reoriented to convert the producer's culture into a consumer's culture. In a society of scarcity, or even of moderate abundance, the productive capacity has barely sufficed to supply the goods which people already desire and which they regard as essential to an adequate standard of living. Hence the social imperative has fallen upon increases in production. But in a society of abundance, the productive capacity can supply new kinds of goods faster than society in the mass learns to crave these goods or to regard them as necessities. If this new capacity is to be used, the imperative must fall upon consumption, and the society must be adjusted to a new set of drives and values in which consumption is paramount.

The implications of the consumer orientation have received consideration from a number of writers, including David Riesman, who, in *The Lonely Crowd*, has described the consumer personality with notable insight. Among such writers, Percival and Paul Goodman, in their study *Communitas*, have, with brilliance and irony, pictured the life of a consumer society in the future. They begin by showing how, when unplanned production entered a phase of violent fluctuations in the 1920's, government responded with a New Deal which embodied a whole series of devices for the planning and stabilization of production. However, they observe, "there is no corresponding planning of consumption. . . . But hand in hand with a planned expanding production, there must be a planned expanding demand. . . . To leave the demand to the improvisations of advertisers is exactly on a par with the unplanned production of 1929." In order to plan an expansion of demand, they suggest, society requires an analysis of "Efficient Consumption," comparable to, though reversing, Veblen's concept of "Efficient Production." When Veblen set up laboriousness, interest in technique, and other productive virtues of the engineers in contradistinction to the restrictive qualities or practices of the capitalists, he was still thinking in terms of a need for more goods. "But," they continue, "the fact is that for at least two decades now it has been not scarcity of production which has kept men in political subjection (ironically enough, it has partly been the insecurity of so-called 'overproduction'); economically, it has been precisely the weakness, rather than the strength, of the consumption attitudes of emulation, ostentation, and sheer wastefulness which have depressed the productivity which is the economist's ideal. Only the instincts unleashed by war have sufficed, under modern conditions, to bring economic salvation.

"Then let us reverse the analysis and suggest how, even in peacetime, men can be as efficiently wasteful as possible. The city which we design on this principle is not only a theoretical solution for the economics which seem to have become official but also springs from the existent moral demands of the people who have crowded into such metropoles as New York."

In the society of consumption, as the Goodmans visualize it, production is only a means to the end of consumption, and therefore satisfaction in the work disappears. The workman accordingly focuses all his demands upon suitable working conditions, short hours, and high wages, so that he may hasten away with sufficient time, wealth, and energy to seek the goals of the consumer. This quest can be carried on "only in a great city. And the chief drive toward such goods is not individual but social. It is imitation and emulation which result in the lively demand. At first, perhaps, it is 'mass comforts' which satisfy cityfolk—these belong to the imitation of each other; but in the end it is luxuries; for these belong to emulation, to what Veblen used to call the 'imputation of superiority.' . . . All this can take place only in a great city. . . . The heart of the city of expanding effective demand is the department store. . . . Here all things are available according to desire—and are on display in order to suggest the desire. The streets are corridors of the department store; for the work of the people must not be quarantined from its cultural meaning."[3]

In their description of the department-store metropolis, the Goodmans have pictured an unlovely utopia, but the utopia, nonetheless, of a consumer society. I have quoted them at some length because of the clarity with which they show the intrinsic nature of a pure consumer culture. But consumer societies, like all other kinds, seem to fall short of their utopias, and we revert to the question how the citizen, in our mixed production-consumption society, can be educated to perform his role as a consumer, especially as a consumer of goods for which he feels no impulse of need. Clearly he must be educated, and the only institution which we have for instilling new needs, for training people to act as consumers, for altering men's values, and thus for hastening their adjustment to potential abundance is advertising. That is why it seems to me valid to regard advertising as distinctively the institution of abundance.

If it is correct to regard advertising in this way, we must recognize at once that we are dealing with a force that is not merely

3. Percival and Paul Goodman, *Communitas* (Chicago: University of Chicago Press, 1947), pp. 60–64, 73.

economic. We are dealing, as I have already suggested, with one of the very limited group of institutions which can properly be called "instruments of social control." These institutions guide the life of the individual by conceiving of him in a distinctive way and encouraging him to conform as far as possible to the concept. For instance, the church, representing the force of religion, conceives of man as an immortal soul; our schools and colleges, representing the force of learning, conceive of him as a being whose behavior is guided by reason; our business and industry, representing the force of the economic free-enterprise system, conceive of him as a productive agent who can create goods or render services that are useful to mankind. Advertising, of course, is committed to none of these views and entertains them only incidentally. Representing as it does the force of a vast productive mechanism seeking outlets for an overwhelming flow of goods, it conceives of man as a consumer. Each institution is distinctive, again, in the qualities to which it appeals and in the character of the reward which it offers: the church appeals to the spirit or conscience of the individual and offers the rewards of salvation and peace of mind; learning appeals to the reason of man and offers the hope of a perfected society from which evils have been eliminated by the application of wisdom; free enterprise appeals to the energies and the capacities of man and offers the rewards of property, personal attainment, and satisfaction in the job. Advertising appeals primarily to the desires, the wants—cultivated or natural—of the individual, and it sometimes offers as its goal a power to command the envy of others by outstripping them in the consumption of goods and services.

To pursue this parallel a step further, one may add that the traditional institutions have tried to improve man and to develop in him qualities of social value, though, of course, these values have not always been broadly conceived. The church has sought to inculcate virtue and consideration of others—the golden rule; the schools have made it their business to stimulate ability and to impart skills; the free-enterprise system has constantly stressed the importance of hard work and the sinfulness of unproductive occupations. And at least two of these institutions, the church and the school, have been very self-conscious about their roles as guardians of the social values and have conducted themselves with a considerable degree of social responsibility.

In contrast with these, advertising has in its dynamics no motivation to seek the improvement of the individual or to impart qualities of social usefulness, unless conformity to material values may be so characterized. And, though it wields an immense social influence, comparable to the influence of religion and learning, it has no social goals and no social responsibility for what it does with its influence, so long as it refrains from palpable violations of truth and decency. It is this lack of institutional responsibility, this lack of inherent social purpose to balance social power, which, I would argue, is a basic cause for concern about the role of advertising. Occasional deceptions, breaches of taste, and deviations from sound ethical conduct are in a sense superficial and are not necessarily intrinsic. Equally, the high-minded types of advertising which we see more regularly than we sometimes realize are also extraneous to an analysis of the basic nature of advertising. What is basic is that advertising, as such, with all its vast power to influence values and conduct, cannot ever lose sight of the fact that it ultimately regards man as a consumer and defines its own mission as one of stimulating him to consume or to desire to consume.

If one can justifiably say that advertising has joined the charmed circle of institutions which fix the values and standards of society and that it has done this without being linked to any of the socially defined objectives which usually guide such institutions in the use of their power, then it becomes necessary to consider with special care the extent and nature of its influence—how far it extends and in what way it makes itself felt.

To do this, it may be well to begin with the budget, for the activity of all major institutions—great churches, great governments, great universities—can be measured in part by what they spend, and, though such measurements are no substitute for qualitative evaluation, they are significant. In political history the importance of the power of the purse is proverbial. I have already said that the amount spent for advertising in the United States in 1951 was $6,548,000,000. Perhaps this may be a little more meaningful if I add that the amount is equivalent to $199 per year for every separate family in the United States. Compare this with what the nation paid for primary and secondary public education in 1949, which amounted to a total expenditure of $5,010,000,000. This means that, for every household, we paid $152. Our national outlay for the education of citizens, therefore, amounted to substantially less than our expenditure for the education of consumers. It would also be interesting to compare the financial strength of advertising and of religion, but, since the churches do not publicize records of their financial operations, I can only remark that there were 180,000 gainfully employed clergymen in the United States in 1950, and most of them were men of very modest incomes. For every clergyman supported by any church, advertising spent $36,000.

Perhaps more explicit comparisons may serve to reinforce this point of the relative magnitude of advertising activities. I will mention two: In 1949–50 the operating expenses of Yale University were $15,000,000; in 1948 the expenses, for newspaper advertising only, of two major distilleries, Schenley and National Distillers, were more than half of this amount, or $7,800,000. In 1944 the major political parties spent $23,000,000 to win the public to the support of Mr. Roosevelt or of Governor Dewey; in 1948, Procter and Gamble, Colgate-Palmolive-Peet, and Lever Brothers spent more than $23,000,000 to win the public to the support of one or another of their products.

With expenditures of this order of magnitude, advertising clearly thrusts with immense impact upon the mass media and, through them, upon the public. The obvious and direct impact is, of course, through the quantity of space it occupies in the newspapers and magazines and the amount of time it occupies in radio and television broadcasts. Either in space or in time the totals are impressive, and, if advertising had no influence upon the information in newspapers, the stories in magazines, and the programs in radio and television, it would still be a force worthy of major consideration because of the influence of the advertising matter itself. But it does have a profound influence upon the media, and for students of American opinion and American life it is important that this influence should be understood.

To appreciate this influence, let us consider the position of most magazines a century ago, as contrasted with their position today. At that time the only financial support which a magazine could expect was from its readers. This meant that, if a person did not care to read, the magazine had no means of appealing to him and no objective in doing so. If editors worried about circulation, it was because they needed more revenue from subscriptions, and if they had enough subscriptions to support them on a modest scale of operations, they could safely proceed on a basis of keeping their standards high and their circulation limited. They did not worry very much about advertising, for the reason that there was not much advertising to worry about. At the time of the Civil War, for instance, it is estimated that the total income from advertising received by all newspapers and periodicals averaged about 25 cents per capita yearly for the population at that time.

Today, of course, these conditions have ceased to apply. Newspapers and magazines no longer look to their subscribers as the major source of revenue. As long ago as 1935 the revenue of all newspapers in the country was $760,000,000, of which $500,000,-000 came from advertising and $260,000,000 from subscriptions. At the same time, the magazines of the United States enjoyed a revenue of $144,000,000 from subscriptions and $186,000,000 from advertising. That is, approximately two out of every three newspaper dollars came from advertising, and more than one out of every two magazine dollars came from the same source. The subscriber had been reduced to a sad position: whereas at one time periodicals had fished for subscribers, they now fished for advertisers and used subscribers as bait. Since that time, newspaper advertising has increased more than threefold, to the total of $2,226,-000,000, and magazine advertising has risen to $562,000,000, from which we may infer that the subscriber is now, more than ever before, a secondary figure. If I may express the same point in a different way, the situation is this: In 1935 American families paid an average of $6.60 a year to receive newspapers, but advertisers paid an average of $12.70 to have newspapers sent to each family, and in 1951 advertising was paying $56 a year to have newspapers delivered to each family. Clearly that was far more than the household itself could possibly be expected to pay. Similarly, with magazines, while subscribers in 1935 were paying $3.60 a year to receive them, advertisers were paying $4.70 to have them sent, and by 1951 American advertising had increased enough to pay $14 per family per year as its stake in the magazines on the living-room table of the American home. In many cases, as of magazines with large advertising sections, the real situation is that the advertiser buys the magazine for the "purchaser," and what the purchaser pays as the "price" of the magazine is really only a kind of qualifying fee to prove that he is a bona fide potential consumer and not a mere deadhead on whom this handsome advertising spread would be wasted.

If this were merely a matter of some magazines being published for consumers and other magazines being published for readers, with the public retaining a choice between the two, the result would not have been quite so sweeping; but the effect of this change has been to threaten with extinction the magazine that is published first and foremost for its readers.

The threat operates in this way: the magazine with large advertising revenue can afford to pay its contributors more, and therefore it can secure better contributors than the magazine which enjoys very little revenue of this kind. In a sense, the advertiser is prepared to buy better authors for the reader than the reader is prepared to buy for himself. But this means automatically that any magazine which wishes to secure or retain the best writers must get advertising. But to get advertising it must also get mass circulation. To get mass circulation it must publish material with a mass appeal. Also, it must keep its subscription costs low, which in turn makes it more dependent than ever upon advertising revenue. At this point a fixed cycle is virtually inescapable: millions of readers are essential to secure a large revenue from advertising, advertising is essential to enable the magazine to sell at a price that will secure millions of readers—therefore, the content of the magazine must be addressed to the millions. Thus the best writers, those who have proved able to write for the most discriminating readers, are put to work writing for consumers who may not be readers at all.

But it is even more significant to realize that other media are far more completely part of the institutional apparatus of advertising than are periodicals. Magazines and newspapers are still paid for in part by the consumer; but radio and television programs are paid for almost wholly by advertisers. In 1951 it was estimated that there were 100,000,000 radios in the United States, and radio advertising was estimated at $690,000,000. That is, advertisers were annually spending $6.90 to provide each set with programs, while the programs received by the 15,000,000 television sets were being subsidized at the rate of $32 a set.

What this means, in functional terms, it seems to me, is that the newspaper feature, the magazine article, the radio program, do not attain the dignity of being ends in themselves; they are rather means to an end: that end, of course, is to catch the reader's attention so that he will then read the advertisement or hear the commercial, and to hold his interest until these essential messages have been delivered. The program or the article becomes a kind of advertisement in itself—becomes the "pitch," in the telling language of the circus barker. Its function is to induce people to accept the commercial, just as the commercial's function is to induce them to accept the product.[4]

A year or two ago an English critic complained of American periodical writing that it "fixes the attention but does not engage the mind." If this is true, it is not because of any intrinsic vacuity on the part of American writers but because the most important financial supporters of such writing are paying for it to do exactly what is alleged. "To fix the attention but not to engage the mind" is a precise statement of the advertiser's formula.

In saying this, I do not mean at all to suggest that advertisers are personally hostile to thoughtful writing or that they consciously desire to encourage writing which has a low intellectual content. On the contrary, it should be recognized that some of the advertising associations have shown themselves soberly aware of the power they wield and acutely desirous of using it for the public good. But it is the nature of advertising that it must aim for a mass appeal, and it is the nature of the mass media that they must present any item—an idea or a fact or a point of view—in such a way that it will attract the maximum number of readers. To do this, of course, they must suppress any controversial or esoteric aspects of the item and must express it in terms of the least common denominator. But these terms are usually emotional ones rather than rational ones, for the emotional impulses of a large group of people are much more uniform throughout the group than are the mental processes of various individuals in the same group. Walter Lippmann expressed this idea very precisely a good many years ago, in his *The Phantom Public*. He was speaking of political action, but his words nevertheless apply to

4. *A Study of Four Media*, published by the Alfred Politz Research Company (1953), states that "the delivery of an audience for the advertiser is the fundamental function of any medium" (p. 5).

all communication which involves masses of people. "Since the general opinions of large numbers of persons," he said, "are almost certain to be a vague and confusing medley, action cannot be taken until these opinions have been factored down, canalized, compressed, and made uniform. The making of one general will out of a multitude of general wishes . . . consists essentially in the use of symbols which assemble emotions after they have been detached from their ideas. . . . The process, therefore, by which general opinions are brought to coöperation consists of an intensification of feeling and a degradation of significance."

Mr. Donald Slesinger, speaking at the University of Chicago some years ago, made a very similar observation in a context which included other matters besides politics. "Since common experience is essential to communication," he said, "the greater the number to be [simultaneously] reached, the simpler the communication must be."[5]

These factors of simplification, of intensifying the feeling while degrading the significance, and of fixing the attention of the mass audience are all related to one basic condition of the media, namely, that they are concerned not with finding an audience to hear their message but rather with finding a message to hold their audience. The prime requisite of the message is that it must not diminish the audience either by antagonizing or by leaving out anyone. Moreover, since the actual personnel and tastes of a vast, amorphous, and "invisible" audience cannot possibly be known, the result is, in effect, to set up an axiom that the message must not say anything that, in the opinion of a cautious proprietor, might *possibly* offend or leave out some of those who might *possibly* form part of the audience. For such an axiom there are several implicit corollaries of far-reaching importance. First, a message must not deal with subjects of special or out-of-the-way

5. Donald Slesinger, "The Film and Public Opinion," in a symposium, *Print, Radio, and Film in a Democracy* (Chicago: University of Chicago Press, 1942), pp. 79, 88.

interest, since such subjects by definition have no appeal for the majority of the audience. Second, it must not deal with any subject at a high level of maturity, since many people are immature, chronologically or otherwise, and a mature level is one which, by definition, leaves such people out. Third, it must not deal with matters which are controversial or even unpleasant or distressing, since such matters may, by definition, antagonize or offend some members of the audience.

If I may examine each of these corollaries briefly, we are confronted first with the fact that many perfectly inoffensive and noncontroversial subjects are excluded from the media simply because these subjects appeal to only a limited number of people. Being directed to the millions, the media must necessarily avoid consideration of subjects which interest only the thousands or the hundreds. This implies a danger to freedom of expression, but not the precise danger against which the guardians of our liberties are usually warning us. They fear that large publishers and advertisers, wielding autocratic power, will ruthlessly suppress minority ideas. The dynamics of the mass market, however, would seem to indicate that freedom of expression has less to fear from the control which large advertisers exercise than from the control which these advertisers permit the mass market to exercise. In the mass media we have little evidence of censorship in the sense of deliberate, planned suppression imposed by moral edict but much evidence of censorship in the sense of operative suppression of a great range of subjects—a suppression imposed by public indifference or, more precisely, by the belief of those who control the media, that the public would be indifferent.[6]

For instance, as Slesinger remarked, motion pictures cannot

6. "In our society the captains of industry and princes of merchandise who, one would have thought, would be the great social initiators, are generally hamstrung in expressing the slightest overt public opinion, for it would be bound to be unpopular with at least a minority; and this would be fatal to sales" (Goodman and Goodman, *op. cit.*, p. 80).

concern themselves with topics that interest only a minority of people. To borrow his illustration, there is no group which would regard treatment of the themes of horticulture or antique-collecting as objectionable, yet, in fact, motion pictures are in effect barred from using these themes, because "the part of the audience that was interested in horticulture might very well be completely bored by the collection of antiques. But both the gardeners and the antique-collectors can readily get together on a kiss in the dark."

Closely related to the exclusion of special subjects is the avoidance of advanced or mature treatment of the subjects which are accepted. Paul F. Lazarsfeld has investigated this aspect of the matter as it manifests itself in connection with radio and has stated his conclusions very pointedly. He speaks of the appearance of a new type of "radio consumer" in many cultural areas. "Radio," he said, writing in 1941, "has helped to bring to the attention of the American people the important events in Europe and thus has contributed to the generally increased interest in news. However, it has been shown in special studies that this new type of news-consumer created by radio has a more hazy knowledge and a less acute interest in those events than the traditional and smaller groups of people with long-established news interests. A similar audience has been developed in the field of serious music. There is no doubt that the broadcasting of good music over hundreds of stations in this country has enlarged the number of those who like it. Still, a more detailed study of their tastes and attitudes has shown that the musical world of these new music lovers is different, if not inferior, to that of the musical elite of past decades and as judged by classical standards."[7]

In a democracy no one should disparage the value of any activity which serves to raise the level of popular taste, but it is still legitimate to count the cost of such a gain. Particularly in

7. Paul F. Lazarsfeld, "The Effects of Radio on Public Opinion," in *Print, Radio, and Film in a Democracy*, pp. 72–73.

connection with news broadcasting and in connection with popular articles on public affairs, it seems to me that we can easily see the application of Walter Lippmann's formula, "the intensification of feeling and the degradation of significance."

Finally, there is the avoidance of the controversial or distressing. This manifests itself not only in connection with obvious matters such as labor unionization, race relations, or the like, but more fundamentally in the creation of a stereotype of society from which all questions of social significance are carefully screened out. Lazarsfeld has made this point, also, very strikingly with radio "soap operas" as his illustration. These programs, numbering nearly three hundred a day ten years ago, are eagerly awaited throughout the nation by millions of women who might certainly be expected "to pattern their own behavior upon the solutions for domestic problems that appear in the serials." But, in fact, Lazarsfeld found that the programs carefully refrained from exercising any such influence: "The settings are middle class—conforming to the environment of the listeners. In forty-five serials carefully followed up for three weeks, not one character was found who came from the laboring class. Inasmuch as they are upper-class characters, they are used to lend glamour to the middle-class settings rather than to play a role of their own. All problems are of an individualistic nature. It is not social forces but the virtues and vices of the central characters that move the events along. People lose jobs not for economic reasons but because their fellow-men lie or are envious. A simple black and white technique avoids any insoluble conflicts. Even the everyday activities of the characters are patterned according to what the listeners presumably do themselves; reading, for instance, is something which is rarely done in these plays. No other effect than the reinforcement of already existing attitudes can be expected from such programs."[8]

In a sense—a negative sense—the desire to offend no one involves an attitude of what may be called "tolerance." As David

8. *Ibid.*, pp. 67–68.

Riesman tellingly remarks, the writer or broadcaster, addressing himself to the amorphous audience, does not know how the virus of indignation may be received, and he must therefore "be preoccupied with the antibodies of tolerance." But, clearly, this tolerance is, as the phrase implies, one of mental asepsis rather than one of mental nourishment. It deals with ideas not by weighing them but by diluting them. Tolerance once implied that the advocates of an idea might be heard without prejudice and judged on their merits, but this toleration merely implies that, since society will refrain from exercising the power to judge them, it will relieve itself of responsibility to hear them. It involves not impartiality of judgment but simply default of judgment.

In the realm of politics, of course, antagonistic points of view do continue to receive a hearing, and the continued presence of vigorously partisan editorials and radio addresses by men in political life may seem to disprove all that I have just been saying; but the significant fact is that the political sector is the only one where the indulgence, or even the recognition, of vigorously maintained viewpoints is permitted. Many social questions, many of the profound problems of American life, lie beyond the pale.

In this discussion of the importance of advertising, the purpose has been to explore its effects upon the noneconomic phases of our culture. For that reason I have refrained from introducing some significant points in connection with the changes wrought by advertising in the economy. For instance, it is important that advertising tends less to provide the consumer with what he wants than to make him like what he gets. In this connection Richard B. Tennant, in his recent book on the American cigarette industry, shows that the American Tobacco Company, in the second decade of this century, produced at least eight different brands of cigarettes, designed to meet the diverse demands of varying smoking tastes and different purses; but after 1925 it began to concentrate its advertising upon Lucky Strikes and after 1927 began to dispose of its minor brands to other companies, though it did later develop Herbert Tareytons and Pall Malls.[9] Also, it is important that advertising tends to minimize information and maximize appeal, with the result that producers tend less to differentiate their products physically, in terms of quality, or economically, in terms of price, than to differentiate them psychologically in terms of slogan, package, or prestige. "How many advertisers," asked Walter Dill Scott in 1903, "describe an undergarment so that the reader can feel the pleasant contact with the body?" Surely this is one question to which time has given us a definite answer.

But the most important effects of this powerful institution are not upon the economics of our distributive system; they are upon the values of our society. If the economic effect is to make the purchaser like what he buys, the social effect is, in a parallel but broader sense, to make the individual like what he gets—to enforce already existing attitudes, to diminish the range and variety of choices, and, in terms of abundance, to exalt the materialistic virtues of consumption.

Certainly it marks a profound social change that this new institution for shaping human standards should be directed, not, as are the school and the church, to the inculcation of beliefs or attitudes that are held to be of social value, but rather to the stimulation or even the exploitation of materialistic drives and emulative anxieties and then to the validation, the sanctioning, and the standardization of these drives and anxieties as accepted criteria of social value. Such a transformation, brought about by the need to stimulate desire for the goods which an abundant economy has to offer and which a scarcity economy would never have produced, offers strong justification for the view that advertising should be recognized as an important social influence and as our newest major institution—an institution peculiarly identified with one of the most pervasive forces in American life, the force of economic abundance.

9. Richard Bremer Tennant, *The American Cigarette Industry* (New Haven: Yale University Press, 1950), pp. 81–84.

IX. Abundance and the Formation of Character

As this analysis draws toward a close, any student of the behavioral sciences who has read this far may quite possibly feel that he has been imposed upon. As far back as chapter ii, I was rash enough to suggest that history and the behavioral sciences might have something to offer, each to the other, in the study of man. In that chapter it was asserted that history has a function in explaining the determinants of culture; the value of history in interpreting national character was asserted, and emphasis was even placed upon the statement of Hans Gerth and C. Wright Mills that "the structural and historical features of modern society must be connected with the most intimate features of man's self."

But then, so the complaint might run, this relation between the public and the private aspects of American life was not really developed. The author, being a student of history, did as might be expected. After superficial lip service to an arresting idea—the idea of working along an important but neglected interdisciplinary frontier—he relapsed into a comfortable historical perspective from which he could examine the kind of topics which historians customarily examine: the quest for equality, the ideal of democracy, the concept of an American mission to redeem the world, the experience of the frontier, and the impact of advertising. What possible value can such discussions have for a behavioral scientist who is trying to find out about the formation of personality or character in an individual infant? This infant—any infant—is the child of specific parents. He lives in a specific place and is exposed not only to his parents but to kinspeople and neighbors and, by the third or fourth year of life, to other small fry whom the psychologist will designate as his "peers." The behavioral scientist wants to know how the circumstances and traits of all these people control their attitudes and behavior toward the infant; in what way they manifest these attitudes and project their own values, their tensions, their orientation, upon the child; and by what process he receives these projections from the outside and internalizes them as part of the character within his own personality. This is what the behavioral scientist means when he talks about the formation of personality or of character. Certainly, therefore, the question arises: What pertinence can such topics as "mobility," "equality," "democracy," "the frontier," or "advertising" have in the kind of investigation that he conducts?

The present chapter seeks to face this question honestly, by attempting to show in direct terms how these generalized and impersonal factors, pertaining to the economy of abundance, do impinge upon the primary conditions in the infancy of an American child. If worth-while links between history and the behavioral sciences really exist, the only conclusive way to establish them will be by showing them fully in this way. But, before proceeding to this attempt, it seems valid to recognize that the general historical factors already discussed and the specific life-experiences which seem critical to the behavioral scientist are not as disparate as they might appear.

Ever since the time of Freud, behavioral scientists have steadily been broadening their conception of the range of external experience which goes into the formation of personality. Freud himself dealt heavily in biological drives and instinctual impulses which were inherent in the individual and did not have to be accounted for by any experience with the external world. Subsequently, however, psychoanalysts like Erich Fromm and Karen Horney recognized that many manifestations which Freud had regarded as universal were, in fact, limited to specific cultures. In the course of time, these revisionists fought and won the battle for recognition of the principle that culture determines personality. But even after this victory many seemed anxious to confine themselves to the narrowest possible segment of the culture. It was generally agreed that "the effects of environmental forces in moulding the personality are, in general, the more profound, the earlier in the life history of the individual they are brought to bear."[1] This premise gave to investigators a sound basis for assigning a very high priority to parent-child relationships and the experiences of infancy, and this priority seems to be altogether valid. But there has been an especially marked tendency in very recent studies to accord more recognition to the broad range of the cultural experience. It was because of this tendency that Haring, in his comparison between the characters of the Japanese of Amami Oshima and the Japanese of Japan proper, makes such an emphatic point of the fact that police tyranny and not infant training seems to be the critical factor in causing the divergence.[2] The same reason led T. W. Adorno, in 1950, to assert the necessity for taking general social and economic conditions into account: "The major influences upon personality development arise in the course of child training as carried forward in a setting of family life. What happens here is profoundly influenced by economic and social factors. It is not only that each family in trying to rear its children proceeds according to the ways of the social, ethnic, and religious groups in which it has membership, but crude economic factors affect directly the parents' behavior toward the child. This means that broad changes in social conditions and institutions will have a direct bearing upon the kinds of personalities that develop within a society."

One of the most striking expressions of this demand for a

1. T. W. Adorno *et al., The Authoritarian Personality* (New York: Harper & Bros., 1950), pp. 5–6.

2. Douglas G. Haring, "Japanese National Character: Cultural Anthropology, Psychoanalysis, and History," *Yale Review,* XLII (1953), 375–92.

broader recognition of the whole gamut of experience has been voiced by Hans Gerth and C. Wright Mills (*Character and Social Structure* [New York: Harcourt, Brace & Co., 1953]), and, though it was quoted previously in chapter ii, it is perhaps of sufficient importance to justify repetition. Their position is that they are not even prepared to concede that the experiences of infancy are crucial without submitting the whole question to intensive study: "We cannot . . . rest content with the assumption that the kinship order, with its tensions of early love and authority, is necessarily the basic and lasting factor in the formation of personality; and that other orders of society are projective systems from this, until we have studied the selection and continued formation of personality in the economic and religious and political institutions of various social structures. The father may not be the *primary* authority, but rather the replica of the power relations of society, and of course, the unwitting transmitter of larger authorities to his spouse and children."

In the light of these statements and others like them and in view also of the factors currently being examined by students of personality, it is now evident that social psychology is steadily reaching out more widely to bring the major tendencies of the political, economic, and social spheres within the range of its analysis. Topics such as "advertising," or "the frontier," or "the democratic ideal" no longer seem so remote from the study of personality as they once appeared.

Also, these topics are not so far removed from "the most intimate features of man's self" as a literal approach to them might indicate. It is true that historical discussion of such topics is usually couched in general or collective terms, so that one thinks of democracy in connection with public decisions; of advertising in connection with the mass media; or of the frontier in connection with the temporary absence of public institutions and services such as law, organized religion, and organized medicine. But all these clearly have their bearings upon the individual in his personal capacity. American ideas of equality, for instance, apply not only politically between fellow-citizens but also within the family, where relations between husband and wife or even between parent and child do not reflect the principle of authority nearly so much as in most countries which share the Western tradition. The frontier exercised many imperatives upon the individual, for it determined rigorously the role which he had to fill: he had to be capable of performing a very wide variety of functions without relying upon anyone else, and he had to exercise his own judgment in deciding when to perform them. From his early youth this was what society required of him. Also, it expected him to show a considerable measure of hardihood, and to do this from childhood, especially if he were a boy. To take the example of advertising, this also trains the individual for a role—the role of a consumer—and it profoundly modifies his system of values, for it articulates the rationale of material values for him in the same way in which the church articulates a rationale of spiritual values.

In the same way, almost all public and general forces can be found operating in the private and individual sphere. Hence it is not at all far-fetched to argue that even a discussion of the general aspect of one of these forces is full of implicit indications which touch the personal lives and the conditioning and response of individuals. Many such indications are intended in the preceding chapters. But, if the utility of the historical approach in an understanding of the factors of personality formation is to be adequately proved, something more than an indirect or implicit relationship must be established. The questions recur: What, if anything, does the factor of abundance have to do with the process of personality formation (in so far as this process is understood) in the United States? How does the process differ from that in countries where the measure of abundance is not so great?

To these questions, I believe, some highly explicit answers are possible. Let us therefore be entirely concrete. Let us consider the situation of a six-month-old American infant, who is not yet aware that he is a citizen, a taxpayer, and a consumer.

This individual is, to all appearances, just a very young specimen of *Homo sapiens*, with certain needs for protection, care, shelter, and nourishment which may be regarded as the universal biological needs of human infancy rather than specific cultural needs. It would be difficult to prove that the culture has as yet differentiated him from other infants, and, though he is an American, few would argue that he has acquired an American character. Yet abundance and the circumstances arising from abundance have already dictated a whole range of basic conditions which, from his birth, are constantly at work upon this child and which will contribute in the most intimate and basic way to the formation of his character.

To begin with, abundance has already revolutionized the typical mode of his nourishment by providing for him to be fed upon cow's milk rather than upon his mother's milk, taken from the bottle rather than from the breast. Abundance contributes vitally to this transformation, because bottle feeding requires fairly elaborate facilities of refrigeration, heating, sterilization, and temperature control, which only an advanced technology can offer and only an economy of abundance can make widely available. I will not attempt here to resolve the debated question as to the psychological effects, for both mother and child, of bottle feeding as contrasted with breast feeding in infant nurture. But it is clear that the changeover to bottle feeding has encroached somewhat upon the intimacy of the bond between mother and child. The nature of this bond is, of course, one of the most crucial factors in the formation of character. Bottle feeding also must tend to emphasize the separateness of the infant as an individual, and thus it makes, for the first time, a point which the entire culture reiterates constantly throughout the life of the average American. In addition to the psychic influences which may be involved in the manner of taking the food, it is also a matter of capital importance that the bottle-fed baby is, on the whole, better nourished than the breast-fed infant and therefore likely to grow more rapidly, to be more vigorous, and to suffer fewer ailments, with whatever effects these physical conditions may have upon his personality.

It may be argued also that abundance has provided a characteristic mode of housing for the infant and that this mode further emphasizes his separateness as an individual. In societies of scarcity, dwelling units are few and hard to come by, with the result that high proportions of newly married young people make their homes in the parental ménage, thus forming part of an "extended" family, as it is called. Moreover, scarcity provides a low ratio of rooms to individuals, with the consequence that whole families may expect as a matter of course to have but one room for sleeping, where children will go to bed in intimate propinquity to their parents. But abundance prescribes a different regime. By making it economically possible for newly married couples to maintain separate households of their own, it has almost destroyed the extended family as an institution in America and has ordained that the child shall be reared in a "nuclear" family, so-called, where his only intimate associates are his parents and his siblings, with even the latter far fewer now than in families of the past. The housing arrangements of this new-style family are suggested by census data for 1950. In that year there were 45,983,000 dwelling units to accommodate the 38,310,000 families in the United States, and, though the median number of persons in the dwelling unit was 3.1, the median number of rooms in the dwelling unit was 4.6. Eighty-four per cent of all dwelling units reported less than one person per room.[3] By providing the ordinary family with more than one room for sleep-

3. Data from United States Department of Commerce, *Census of Housing: 1950*, Vol. I, Part I (Washington: Government Printing Office, 1953), p. xxx. For purposes of enumeration kitchens were counted as rooms, but bathrooms, hallways, and pantries were not. Many dwelling units were, of course, occupied by single persons or others not falling under the definition of a family, but the number of households—43,468,000—was also less than the number of dwelling units.

ing, the economy thus produces a situation in which the child will sleep either in a room alone or in a room shared with his brothers or sisters. Even without allowing for the cases in which children may have separate rooms, these conditions mean that a very substantial percentage of children now sleep in a room alone, for, with the declining birth rate, we have reached a point at which an increasing proportion of families have one child or two children rather than the larger number which was at one time typical. For instance, in the most recent group of mothers who had completed their childbearing phase, according to the census, 19.5 per cent had had one child and 23.4 had had two. Thus almost half of all families with offspring did not have more than two children throughout their duration. In the case of the first group, all the children were "only" children throughout their childhood, and in the second group half of the children were "only" children until the second child was born. To state this in another, and perhaps a more forcible, way, it has been shown that among American women who arrived at age thirty-four during the year 1949 and who had borne children up to that time, 26.7 per cent had borne only one child, and 34.5 per cent had borne only two.[4] If these tendencies persist, it would mean that, among families where there are children, hardly one in three will have more than two children.

The census has, of course, not got around to finding out how the new-style family, in its new-style dwelling unit, adjusts the life-practice to the space situation. But it is significant that America's most widely circulated book on the care of infants advises

4. Clyde V. Kiser, "Fertility Trends in the United States," *Journal of the American Statistical Association*, XLVII (1952), 31–33. Figures given by Kiser, based on research by P. K. Whelpton, also include childless women; but my concern here is with the sibling relationships of children and not with the fertility of women, and I have therefore based my statements upon the record of women who have borne children rather than upon women of childbearing age. My statement has no way of allowing for half-brothers and sisters born of different mothers or for differentiating the number of children who survive from the number born.

that "it is preferable that he [the infant] not sleep in his parents' room after he is about 12 months old," offers the opinion that "it's fine for each [child] to have a room of his own, if that's possible," and makes the sweeping assertion that "it's a sensible rule not to take a child into the parents' bed for any reason."[5] It seems clear beyond dispute that the household space provided by the economy of abundance has been used to emphasize the separateness, the apartness, if not the isolation, of the American child.

Not only the nourishment and housing, but also the clothing of the American infant are controlled by American abundance. For one of the most sweeping consequences of our abundance is that, in contrast to other peoples who keep their bodies warm primarily by wearing clothes, Americans keep their bodies warm primarily by a far more expensive and even wasteful method: namely, by heating the buildings in which they are sheltered. Every American who has been abroad knows how much lighter is the clothing—especially the underclothing—of Americans than of people in countries like England and France, where the winters are far less severe than ours, and every American who can remember the conditions of a few decades ago knows how much lighter our clothing is than that of our grandparents. These changes have occurred because clothing is no longer the principal device for securing warmth. The oil furnace has not only displaced the open fireplace; it has also displaced the woolen undergarment and the vest.

This is a matter of considerable significance for adults but of far greater importance to infants, for adults discipline themselves to wear warm garments, submitting, for instance, to woolen underwear more or less voluntarily. But the infant knows no such discipline, and his garments or bedclothes must be kept upon him by forcible means. Hence primitive people, living in

5. Benjamin Spock, *The Pocket Book of Baby and Child Care* (New York: Pocket Books, Inc., 1946), pp. 96–97.

outdoor conditions, swaddle the child most rigorously, virtually binding him into his clothes, and breaking him to them almost as a horse is broken to the harness. Civilized peoples mitigate the rigor but still use huge pins or clips to frustrate the baby's efforts to kick off the blankets and free his limbs. In a state of nature, cold means confinement and warmth means freedom, so far as young humans are concerned. But abundance has given the American infant physical freedom by giving him physical warmth in cold weather.

In this connection it may be surmised that abundance has also given him a permissive system of toilet training. If our forebears imposed such training upon the child and we now wait for him to take the initiative in these matters himself, it is not wholly because the former held a grim Calvinistic doctrine of child-rearing that is philosophically contrary to ours. The fact was that the circumstances gave them little choice. A mother who was taking care of several babies, keeping them clean, making their clothes, washing their diapers in her own washtub, and doing this, as often as not, while another baby was on the way, had little choice but to hasten their fitness to toilet themselves. Today, on the contrary, the disposable diaper, the diaper service, and most of all the washing machine, not to mention the fact that one baby seldom presses upon the heels of another, make it far easier for the mother to indulge the child in a regime under which he will impose his own toilet controls in his own good time.

Thus the economy of plenty has influenced the feeding of the infant, his regime, and the physical setting within which he lives. These material conditions alone might be regarded as having some bearing upon the formation of his character, but the impact of abundance by no means ends at this point. In so far as it has an influence in determining what specific individuals shall initiate the infant into the ways of man and shall provide him with his formative impressions of the meaning of being a person, it must be regarded as even more vital. When it influences the nature of the relationships between these individuals and the infant, it must be recognized as reaching to the very essence of the process of character formation.

The central figures in the dramatis personae of the American infant's universe are still his parents, and in this respect, of course, there is nothing peculiar either to the American child or to the child of abundance. But abundance has at least provided him with parents who are in certain respects unlike the parents of children born in other countries or born fifty years ago. To begin with, it has given him young parents, for the median age of fathers at the birth of the first child in American marriages (as of 1940) was 25.3 years, and the median age of mothers was 22.6 years. This median age was substantially lower than it had been in the United States in 1890 for both fathers and mothers. Moreover, as the size of families has been reduced and the wife no longer continues to bear a succession of children throughout the period of her fertility, the median age of mothers at the birth of the last child has declined from 32 years (1890) to 27 years (1940). The age of the parents at the birth of both the first child and the last child is far lower than in the case of couples in most European countries. There can be little doubt that abundance has caused this differential, in the case of the first-born by making it economically possible for a high proportion of the population to meet the expenses of homemaking at a fairly early age. In the case of the last-born, it would also appear that one major reason for the earlier cessation of child-bearing is a determination by parents to enjoy a high standard of living themselves and to limit their offspring to a number for whom they can maintain a similar standard.

By the very fact of their youth, these parents are more likely to remain alive until the child reaches maturity, thus giving him a better prospect of being reared by his own mother and father. This prospect is further reinforced by increases in the life-span, so that probably no child in history has ever enjoyed so strong a likelihood that his parents will survive to rear him. Abundance has produced this situation by providing optimum conditions for prolonging life. But, on the other hand, abundance has also contributed much to produce an economy in which the mother is no longer markedly dependent upon the father, and this change in the economic relation between the sexes has probably done much to remove obstacles to divorce. The results are all too familiar. During the decade 1940–49 there were 25.8 divorces for every 100 marriages in the United States, which ratio, if projected over a longer period, would mean that one marriage out of four would end in divorce. But our concern here is with a six-month-old child, and the problem is to know whether this factor of divorce involves childless couples predominantly or whether it is likely to touch him. The answer is indicated by the fact that, of all divorces granted in 1948, no less than 42 per cent were to couples with children under eighteen, and a very large proportion of these children were of much younger ages. Hence one might say that the economy of abundance has provided the child with younger parents who chose their role of parenthood deliberately and who are more likely than parents in the past to live until he is grown, but who are substantially less likely to preserve the unbroken family as the environment within which he shall be reared.

In addition to altering the characteristics of the child's parents, it has also altered the quantitative relationship between him and his parents. It has done this, first of all, by offering the father such lucrative opportunities through work outside the home that the old agricultural economy in which children worked alongside their fathers is now obsolete. Yet, on the other hand, the father's new employment gives so much more leisure than his former work that the child may, in fact, receive considerably more of his father's attention. But the most vital transformation is in the case of the mother. In the economy of scarcity which controlled the modes of life that were traditional for many centuries, an upper-class child was reared by a nurse, and all others were normally reared by their mothers. The scarcity economy could not support many nonproductive members, and these mothers, though not "employed," were most decidedly hard workers, busily engaged in cooking, washing, sewing, weaving, preserving, caring for the henhouse, the garden, and perhaps the cow, and in general carrying on the domestic economy of a large family. Somehow they also attended to the needs of a numerous brood of children, but the mother was in no sense a full-time attendant upon any one child. Today, however, the economy of abundance very nearly exempts a very large number of mothers from the requirement of economic productivity in order that they may give an unprecedented share of their time to the care of the one or two young children who are now the usual number in an American family. Within the home, the wide range of labor-saving devices and the assignment of many functions, such as laundering, to service industries have produced this result. Outside the home, employment of women in the labor force has steadily increased, but the incidence of employment falls upon unmarried women, wives without children, and wives with grown children. In fact, married women without children are two and one-half times as likely to be employed as those with children. Thus what amounts to a new dispensation has been established for the child. If he belongs to the upper class, his mother has replaced his nurse as his full-time attendant. The differences in character formation that might result from this change alone could easily be immense. To mention but one possibility, the presence of the nurse must inevitably have made the child somewhat aware of his class status, whereas the presence of the mother would be less likely to have this effect. If the child does not belong to the upper class, mother and child now impinge upon each other in a relationship whose intensity is of an entirely different magnitude from that which prevailed in the past. The mother has fewer physical distractions in the care of the child, but she is more likely to be restive in her maternal role because it takes her away from attractive employment with which it cannot be reconciled.

If abundance has thus altered the relationship of the child with his parent, it has even more drastically altered the rest of his social milieu, for it has changed the identity of the rest of the personnel who induct him into human society. In the extended family of the past, a great array of kinspeople filled his cosmos and guided him to maturity. By nature, he particularly needed association with children of his own age (his "peers," as they are called), and he particularly responded to the values asserted by these peers. Such peers were very often his brothers and sisters, and, since they were all members of his own family, all came under parental control. This is to say that, in a sense, the parents controlled the peer group, and the peer group controlled the child. The point is worth making because we frequently encounter the assertion that parental control of the child has been replaced by peer-group control; but it is arguable that what is really the case is that children were always deeply influenced by the peer group and that parents have now lost their former measure of control over this group, since it is no longer a familial group. Today the nursery school replaces the large family as a peer group, and the social associations, even of young children, undergo the same shift from focused contact with family to diffused contact with a miscellany of people, which John Galsworthy depicted for grown people in the three novels of the *Forsyte Saga*. Again, the effects upon character may very well be extensive.

Abundance, then, has played a critical part in revolutionizing both the physical circumstances and the human associations which surround the American infant and child. These changes alone would warrant the hypothesis that abundance has profoundly affected the formation of character for such a child.

But to extend this inquiry one step further, it may be worth while to consider how these altered conditions actually impinge upon the individual. Here, of course, is an almost unlimited field for investigation, and I shall only attempt to indicate certain crucial points at which abundance projects conditions that are basic in the life of the child.

One of these points concerns the cohesive force which holds the family together. The family is the one institution which touches all members of society most intimately, and it is perhaps the only social institution which touches young children directly. The sources from which the family draws its strength are, therefore, of basic importance. In the past, these sources were, it would seem, primarily economic. For agrarian society, marriage distinctively involved a division of labor. Where economic opportunity was narrowly restricted, the necessity for considering economic ways and means in connection with marriage led to the arrangement of matches by parents and to the institution of the dowry. The emotional bonds of affection, while always important, were not deemed paramount, and the ideal of romantic love played little or no part in the lives of ordinary people. Where it existed at all, it was as an upper-class luxury. (The very term "courtship" implies this upper-class orientation.) This must inevitably have meant that the partners in the majority of marriages demanded less from one another emotionally than do the partners of romantic love and that the emotional factor was less important to the stability of the marriage. Abundance, however, has played its part in changing this picture. On the American frontier, where capital for dowries was as rare as opportunity for prosperous marriage was plentiful, the dowry became obsolete. Later still, when abundance began to diminish the economic duties imposed upon the housewife, the function of marriage as a division of labor ceased to seem paramount, and the romantic or emotional factor assumed increasing importance. Abundance brought the luxury of romantic love within the reach of all, and, as it did so, emotional harmony became the principal criterion of success in a marriage, while lack of such harmony became a major threat to the existence of the marriage. The statistics of divorce give us a measure of the loss of durability in marriage, but they give us no measure of the factors of instability in the marriages which endure and no measure of the increased focus upon emotional satisfactions in such marriages. The children of enduring marriages, as well as the children of divorce, must inevitably feel the impact of this increased emphasis upon emotional factors, must inevitably sense the difference in the foundations of the institution which holds their universe in place.

In the rearing of a child, it would be difficult to imagine any factors more vital than the distinction between a permissive and an authoritarian regime or more vital than the age at which economic responsibility is imposed. In both these matters the modern American child lives under a very different dispensation from children in the past. We commonly think of these changes as results of our more enlightened or progressive or humanitarian ideas. We may even think of them as results of developments in the specific field of child psychology, as if the changes were simply a matter of our understanding these matters better than our grandparents. But the fact is that the authoritarian discipline of the child, within the authoritarian family, was but an aspect of the authoritarian social system that was linked with the economy of scarcity. Such a regime could never have been significantly relaxed within the family so long as it remained diagnostic in the society. Nor could it have remained unmodified within the family, once society began to abandon it in other spheres.

Inevitably, the qualities which the parents inculcate in a child will depend upon the roles which they occupy themselves. For the ordinary man the economy of scarcity has offered one role, as Simon N. Patten observed many years ago, and the economy of abundance has offered another. Abundance offers "work calling urgently for workmen"; scarcity found the "worker seeking humbly any kind of toil."[6] As a suppliant to his superiors, the worker under scarcity accepted the principle of authority; he accepted his own subordination and the obligation to cultivate the qualities appropriate to his subordination, such as submissiveness, obedience, and deference. Such a man naturally transferred the principle of authority into his own family and, through this principle, instilled into his children the qualities appropriate to people of their kind—submissiveness, obedience, and deference. Many copybook maxims still exist to remind us of the firmness of childhood discipline, while the difference between European and American children—one of the most clearly recognizable of all national differences—serves to emphasize the extent to which Americans have now departed from this firmness.

This new and far more permissive attitude toward children has arisen, significantly, in an economy of abundance, where work has called urgently for the workman. In this situation, no longer a suppliant, the workman found submissiveness no longer a necessity and therefore no longer a virtue. The principle of authority lost some of its majesty, and he was less likely to regard it as the only true criterion of domestic order. In short, he ceased to impose it upon his children. Finding that the most valuable trait in himself was a capacity for independent decision and self-reliant conduct in dealing with the diverse opportunities which abundance offered him, he tended to encourage this quality in his children. The irresponsibility of childhood still called for a measure of authority on one side and obedience on the other, but this became a means to an end and not an end in itself. On the whole, permissive training, to develop independent ability, even though it involves a certain sacrifice of

6. Simon Nelson Patten, *The New Basis of Civilization* (New York: Macmillan Co., 1907), pp. 187–88. I am indebted to Arthur Schlesinger, Jr., for calling my attention to Patten's important observations on this subject.

obedience and discipline, is the characteristic mode of child-rearing in the one country which most distinctively enjoys an economy of abundance. Here, in a concrete way, one finds something approaching proof for Gerth and Mills's suggestion that the relation of father and child may have its importance not as a primary factor but rather as a "replica of the power relations of society."

If scarcity required men to "seek humbly any kind of toil," it seldom permitted women to seek employment outside the home at all. Consequently, the woman was economically dependent upon, and, accordingly, subordinate to, her husband or her father. Her subordination reinforced the principle of authority within the home. But the same transition which altered the role of the male worker has altered her status as well, for abundance "calling urgently for workmen" makes no distinctions of gender, and, by extending economic independence to women, has enabled them to assume the role of partners rather than of subordinates within the family. Once the relation of voluntarism and equality is introduced between husband and wife, it is, of course, far more readily extended to the relation between parent and child.

If abundance has fostered a more permissive regime for the child, amid circumstances of democratic equality within the family, it has no less certainly altered the entire process of imposing economic responsibility upon the child, hence the process of preparing the child for such responsibility. In the economy of scarcity, as I have remarked above, society could not afford to support any substantial quota of nonproductive members. Consequently, the child went to work when he was as yet young. He attended primary school for a much shorter school year than the child of today; only a minority attended high school; and only the favored few attended college. Even during the brief years of schooling, the child worked, in the home, on the farm, or even in the factory. But today the economy of abundance can afford to maintain a substantial proportion of the population in nonproductive status, and it assigns this role, sometimes against their will, to its younger and its elder members. It protracts the years of schooling, and it defers responsibilities for an unusually long span. It even enforces laws setting minimal ages for leaving school, for going to work, for consenting to sexual intercourse, or for marrying. It extends the jurisdiction of juvenile courts to the eighteenth or the twentieth year of age.

Such exemption from economic responsibility might seem to imply a long and blissful youth free from strain for the child. But the delays in reaching economic maturity are not matched by comparable delays in other phases of growing up. On the contrary, there are many respects in which the child matures earlier. Physically, the child at the lower social level will actually arrive at adolescence a year or so younger than his counterpart a generation ago, because of improvement in standards of health and nutrition.[7] Culturally, the child is made aware of the allurements of sex at an earlier age, partly by his familiarity with the movies, television, and popular magazines, and partly by the practice of "dating" in the early teens. By the standards of his peer group, he is encouraged to demand expensive and mature recreations, similar to those of adults, at a fairly early age. By reason of the desire of his parents that he should excel in the mobility race and give proof during his youth of the qualities which will make him a winner in later life, he is exposed to the stimuli of competition before he leaves the nursery. Thus there is a kind of imbalance between the postponement of responsibility and the quickening of social maturity which may have contributed to make American adolescence a more difficult age than human biology alone would cause it to be. Here, again, there are broad implications for the formation of character, and here, again, abundance is at work on both sides of the equa-

7. Alfred C. Kinsey *et al.*, *Sexual Behavior in the Human Male* (Philadelphia: W. B. Saunders Co., 1948), p. 397.

tion, for it contributes as much to the hastening of social maturity as it does to the prolongation of economic immaturity.

Some of these aspects of the rearing of children in the United States are as distinctively American, when compared with other countries, as any Yankee traits that have ever been attributed to the American people. In the multiplicity which always complicates social analysis, such aspects of child-rearing might be linked with a number of factors in American life. But one of the more evident and more significant links, it would seem certain, is with the factor of abundance. Such a tie is especially pertinent in this discussion, where the intention of the whole book has been to relate the study of character, as the historian would approach it, to the same subject as it is viewed by the behavioral scientist. In this chapter, especially, the attempt has been made to throw a bridge between the general historical force of economic abundance and the specific behavioral pattern of people's lives. Historical forces are too often considered only in their public and over-all effects, while private lives are interpreted without sufficient reference to the historical determinants which shape them. But no major force at work in society can possibly make itself felt at one of these levels without also having its impact at the other level. In view of this fact, the study of national character should not stand apart, as it has in the past, from the study of the process of character formation in the individual. In view of this fact, also, the effect of economic abundance is especially pertinent. For economic abundance is a factor whose presence and whose force may be clearly and precisely recognized in the most personal and intimate phases of the development of personality in the child. Yet, at the same time, the presence and the force of this factor are recognizable with equal certainty in the whole broad, general range of American experience, American ideals, and American institutions. At both levels, it has exercised a pervasive influence in the shaping of the American character.

Index

Index

Infant-training: effect of, in character formation, 49, 65, 66, 191; effect of abundance upon, 194–207; *see also* Character formation
Inner-directed man: discussed, 51–53; scarcity and, 70
Institutions: social forces and, 166–67; advertising among, 176
Internal improvements, and abundance, 124
Interstate Commerce Commission, 121
Ivory soap, 170

Jackson, Andrew, 152
Jameson, J. Franklin, 112 n.
Japan, national character of, 14; effect of police system as determinant of, 66, 191
Jefferson, Thomas, 128–29, 138, 152
Jews, and concept of chosen people, 21
John Bull's Other Island, 113–14
Jowett, Benjamin, 5 n.

Kane, Murray, 143, 144 n.
Kardiner, Abram, 36, 39–40, 63
Kinsey, Alfred C., 207
Kiser, Clyde V., 196 n.
Klineberg, Otto, 31 n., 40
Kluckhohn, Clyde, 37, 41, 47
Kohn, Hans, 10, 19
Kossuth, Louis, 130

Labour Party, 118
Lafayette, Marquis de, 129
La Follette, Philip, 156
Laissez faire, 123–26; *see also* Individualism
Lamartine, Alphonse de, 6
Latin-American independence, American sympathy for, 130, 138
Lazarsfeld, Paul, 185, 186
Liberty, relation of, to equality, 92
Lincoln, Abraham, 127, 130
Linton, Ralph: quoted, xviii, xix, 35, 42, 63; contribution of, to study of

national character, 39–40; on personality norms, 44–45
Lippmann, Walter, 182, 186
Loman, Willy, 52
Long, Huey P., 119
"Lost generation," 24
Luce, Henry, 168
Lundberg, Isabel Cary, 135–36
Lynd, Helen, 100
Lynd, Robert, 100

McCormick reaper, 139
McKinley Tariff, 138
Magazines, effects of advertising upon, 167–71, 179–80; *see also* Mass media
Malin, James C., 143, 144 n., 147 n., 157 n.
Man: need of understanding of nature of, xv–xvii; assumptions about, by historians, xv–xvii; assumptions about, by other scholars, xvii, xviii; science of, xviii; history and behavioral studies in science of, xix; nature of, ignored by environmentalists, 24
Marconi, Marchese Guglielmo, 168
Marston, John, 78
Mass media: influence of advertising upon, 167–68, 169–70, 179–87; statistics of, 179–80, 181; social consequences of advertising control of, 181–87
Mead, Margaret, 31 n., 58, 72, 97, 101; and culture configurations, 39, 46; affirms validity of national character, 40; lists approaches to national character, 46 n.; analysis of American character by, 47–50; competition as factor in analysis by, 59; immigrant hypothesis of, criticized, 61–62; applicability of abundance to analysis by, 67–69
Merton, Robert K., 63, 114
Middle class: traits of, in American character, 18; importance of, in America, 100
Mill, John Stuart, 15, 26

DATE DUE

MR 2 9 '78			
JA 1 '94			
APR 4 '95			
AP 05 '00			
NO 08 '06			
GAYLORD			PRINTED IN U.S.A.